How To Make A Speech

STEVE ALLEN

How To Make A Speech

McGraw-Hill Book Company

New York   St. Louis   San Francisco   Hamburg   Mexico   Toronto

1 2 3 4 5 6 7 8 9 F G R F G R 8 7 6 5

ISBN 0-07-001164-8

LIBRARY OF CONGRESS CATALOGING IN PUBLICATION DATA

Allen, Steve, 1921-
How to make a speech.
1. Public speaking.   I. Title.
PN4121.A58   1986   808.5'1   85-13298
ISBN 0-07-001164-8

BOOK DESIGN BY PATRICE FODERO

46 8438

To Jayne, the speaker of the house

Acknowledgments

So far as my office staff is concerned, the fun part of book writing—conceiving the ideas, dictating the text—are reserved for myself. The drudgery, which consists of transcribing audiocassettes, then typing and retyping a series of "final" versions—has been very competently attended to by Loretta Lynn and Ethel Saylor.

I am grateful, too, to my secretary, Dawn Berry, who, by the act of keeping track of my daily appointments and propelling me toward them, keeps my mental tables clear to concentrate on creative work.

When my literary agent, Pat Delahunt, first told me about PJ Haduch, of McGraw-Hill, he said, "You'll find that she doesn't just go through the motions. She's an editor who really digs into a manuscript and makes a great many helpful suggestions."

Delahunt was absolutely right about that.

Lastly, I am indebted to Ellen LaBarbera for her editorial recommendations.

Contents

Human Options

The area in which a poor education shows up first is in self-expression, oral or written. It makes little difference how many university courses or degrees a person may own. If he cannot use words to move an idea from one point to another, his education is incomplete. The business of assembling the right words, putting them down in proper sequence, enabling each one to pull its full weight in the conveyance of meaning—these are the essentials. A school is where these essentials would feel at home.

The first purpose of education is to enable a person to speak up and be understood. Incoherence is no virtue. Feeble language is the surest reflection of a feeble mentality. Even as an affectation rather than a basic condition, stereotyped inarticulateness tends to slow down and cheapen the entire verbal faculty. The trouble with four-letter words and foul language is not so much that they are offensive as that they are weak precisely at the points where they are supposed to be strong. Through incessant, indiscriminate use, they lose their starch and produce a flabbiness in the total effect. They devitalize everything they touch.

Not everyone is lucky enough to be wealthy. But no one need be impoverished in language, nor need anyone be deprived of the distinction that comes from using words with strength and grace. The English language may not be as suitable as the German for scientific purposes, especially in medicine; and it may not have the suppleness and music of French; but in range, depth, and precision it is unsurpassed by any other Western language.

Through the centuries, the refinement of language has become one of the prime achievements of the human mind, thanks largely to people who regarded the creative use of words as the ultimate art. As a result, English has never been static; it has been constantly tested, refined, and enriched. At times, it has suffered the ordeal of regression. The present age may be one of those bleak periods. This, then, is the time for all lovers of the language to recognize that it is in trouble and to make an effort, a very special effort, to give it the attention it requires.

—Norman Cousins

Chapter 1

Overcoming Stage Fright

The brain starts working the moment you are born and never stops until you stand up to speak in public

—Anonymous

It may seem strange that in a text whose purpose is to offer instruction in the art of preparing and delivering speeches I start by taking up the matter of stage fright. I do so because this one factor prevents a good many people from even making the attempt to deliver a talk, in however casual a setting. And even the great majority of those who do try are made miserable by one degree of fear or another during the early stages of their experience. It is not entirely accurate, by the way, to refer to the psychological phenomenon as *stage* fright; this implies that it occurs only when one is on a stage or standing at a speaker's lectern. The fear, in fact, often starts at the moment the possibility of making a speech is first considered—and, oddly, usually lessens once the task is begun. That, then, is the reason the matter should be taken up at the beginning, because it is often the first part of the speaker's personal experience.

Just because you're going to have to deal with the factor of nervousness, I wouldn't want this observation itself to start your knees knocking. According to Daniel Goleman (*The New York Times*, December 18, 1984) social anxiety, in various forms, is epidemic.

"About 40 percent of Americans think of themselves as shy, while only 20 percent say they've never suffered from shyness at some point in their lives," Goleman states. Stage fright, in my view, is simply shyness that relates to formal public appearances.

Because, in the context of this problem, you're probably thinking chiefly of yourself, you may not have given enough attention to the phrase *the great majority* in the above first paragraph. Whether misery loves company I'm not sure, but there is some comfort in knowing that we are not alone with our problems. When we can be assured that most of the human race shares one uncomfortable experience or another, we feel somewhat less anxious about our discomforts. To repeat, almost everyone becomes psychologically and even physically uneasy at the prospect of having to get up in front of an audience. First the good news: You'll get over it. And facing up to the reality of it does help.

The first time I had to address an audience I was in the sixth grade. The assignment was nothing more difficult than having to go to a room across the hall and give a short speech to the members of another class. I literally became physically ill. Nausea, dizziness, clammy palms, and weak knees were the primary symptoms. Fortunately it was never that difficult again. And years later, after I had worked for some time in radio and television, I was conscious of practically no nervousness at all when walking on stage.

There are some rare entertainers who, despite years of success, never resolve the problem. Red Skelton reportedly throws up before every one of his shows, and the great John Barrymore was said to have been a nervous wreck before performing. But such people are the exception.

Now, there is at least a certain reasonableness to the nervousness of actors performing in a play before live audiences. They are troubled by a very specific worry: that they will suddenly go glassy-eyed and forget their lines. In the context of the average speech there need be no such fear. If you don't recall a particular line you had intended to say, you can replace it with another. The audience will be none the wiser.

Fear, of course, is notoriously indifferent to rational argument. If humans were constructed otherwise, every phobia in the world could be dealt with by about five minutes of commonsense reasoning. If you had a true phobia about speaking in public, however, you wouldn't have purchased this book in the first place. The chances are you're like practically all the rest of the human race—perfectly capable, in time, of standing up and speaking to a group, large or small, without suffering a nervous breakdown.

More good news: Even within each individual performance it gets easier as you go along. The worst few moments are usually those just before your entrance or introduction. There is, however, something about hearing your own voice and seeing that the audience does not rise at once and leave the room that restores your sagging confidence. The first thing to do about this particular problem, then, is to relax. You've been speaking all your life anyway, and it's really not that much more difficult on a platform than it is at home, in a rowboat, or on a park bench.

Back in the early 1940s I overcame a moderate fear of flying on airplanes by simply reminding myself that old women and children were even then flying all over the country and that as a healthy male adult I ought to be able to deal with something that came so easily to grandmothers and toddlers. Well, children, grandmothers, the physically handicapped, and all sorts of others have been making speeches for unknown centuries. If they can do it, so can you—so take it easy.

Your nervousness may grow out of your feeling that you do not have a particularly resonant or melodious voice. Consider, then, editor and author Norman Cousins, one of the most effective speakers of our time. He does not have a deep, resonant voice. There is nothing of the formal debater about him, nothing of the great orator. He does not have the practiced, actorish, smile-a-lot-and-look-sincere speaking style of a Ronald Reagan. During the first few minutes of one of his talks, therefore, he may not seem to be an especially effective speaker. But the initial impression is deceptive. Very shortly you become properly tuned in to the importance of what he is saying, sensitive to the essential reasonableness, the wisdom of his observations. You realize then that he is an excellent speaker indeed, despite the lack of vocal melody, and even—on certain words—the faint suggestion of a lisp. You become aware of a remarkable sincerity, a conviction, and—at moments—a passionate intensity.

Cousins' example suggests that it is by no means necessary to have impressive natural gifts as a lecturer. The important factor is communication—enlisting, by whatever means, the concentrated attention of your audience. This Norman does superbly, and so can you, in time and with practice. Grasping this simple point is also helpful in diminishing stage fright.

On the subject of nervousness, consider these autobiographical comments by Margaret Sanger, the courageous woman whose speeches on population control literally changed the world.

Once Amos Pinchot asked me how long it had taken me to prepare the first lecture I delivered on my three months' trip across the country in 1916.

"About fourteen years," I answered. I was thinking of all the time that had passed during which experiences, tragic and stirring, had come to me and were embodied therein.

So much depended on this speech; the women of leisure must be made to listen, the women of wealth to give, the women of influence to protest . . . But the anxiety that went into the composition of the speech was as nothing to the agonies with which I contemplated its utterance. My mother used to say a decent woman only had her name in the papers three times during her life—when she was born, when she married, and when she died. Although by nature I shrank from publicity, the kind of work I had undertaken did not allow me to shirk it—but I was frightened to death. Hoping that practice would give me greater confidence, I used to climb to the roof of the Lexington Avenue Hotel where I was staying and recite, my voice going out over the house tops and echoing timidly among the chimney pots.

I repeated the lecture over and over to myself before I tried it on a small audience in New Rochelle. I did not dare to cut myself adrift from my notes; I had to read it, and when I had finished, did not feel it had been very successful.

By the time I reached Pittsburgh, my first large city, I had memorized every period and comma, but I was still scared that if I lost one word I would not know what the next was. I closed my eyes and spoke in fear and trembling. *The laborers and social workers who crowded the big theatre responded so enthusiastically that I was at least sure their attention had been held by its contents.* [Italics added.]

The point is that you have illustrious company in your anticipatory misery. The majority of eventually eloquent statesmen, religious leaders, and educators have acknowledged that their first few attempts to address audiences were unnerving experiences. In the process of doing research on Mahatma Gandhi for the Public Broadcasting Service's television series *Meeting of Minds*, I came across the information that the great Indian leader—one of the most esteemed men who ever lived and one who accomplished much of his great work by public speaking—was as a young man so inept at the task that he was literally unwilling to speak even in small meetings. Certainly few men have had more effect on the course of history, but observe what William L. Shirer has to say in his *Gandhi Memoir*:

I would see Hitler wildly acclaimed by a mass of 2,000,000 Germans at the Nuremburg party rally. But that meeting was staged, the audience captive. The great crowds all over India that came on their own to hail Gandhi were unorganized and therefore sometimes disorderly, milling about in their excitement at merely being in the presence of the Mahatma. The Germans I saw in Nazi time were deeply moved by the masterful oratory of Hitler. *Gandhi was not an orator. He scarcely raised his voice and made no gestures.* [Italics added.]

Gandhi, of course, was expressing an idea whose time had come: the right of the people of India to be free of the yoke of the British invaders. He also provided religious and philosophical inspiration to his fellow Indians. But again, his example demonstrates that it is not necessary to have a melodious voice, to make dramatic gestures, or to speak with literary grace to affect an audience. If it is evident that you are sincere about the ideas you express, if you know what you're talking about, you can be effective at the lectern, even in the absence of innate rhetorical gifts or in the presence of stage fright.

One fortunate discovery you will make is that you can begin dealing with the problem of fear of public speaking even before you make your first speech. This is possible because during your preparatory period—the time when you are writing your speech, rehearsing it, and training for your forthcoming appearance—the exercises you do, the act of rehearsing itself, can do much to alleviate your apprehension.

Abraham Lincoln, Benjamin Disraeli, Charles Parnell, the Irish leader—all learned the business simply by doing it. You can too.

The reason you are nervous is that you are thinking more of yourself than of what you are going to say. This suggests another partial solution to the problem: Concentrate your attention on the subject of your talk. Be concerned with your message. *Care* about it. Think consciously about the first few points you want to bring out. If you have notes, inspect them. If you have typewritten pages, check once again to see that they are in proper numerical order. Make last-minute underlines or notations. In other words, do something to take your concentration off yourself. The factor of being sincerely interested in what you are saying is crucial. A colleague of the eighteenth-century Scottish economist Adam Smith, the founding philosopher of the free enterprise system, says that when the young Smith was teaching moral philosophy at the University of Glasgow his manner of speaking was quiet and unaffected but that "as he seemed to be *always interested in the subject, he never failed to interest his hearers.*" [Italics added.]

But do not be dismayed if, after all such efforts, you still feel a bit ill at ease. Your feeling of uneasiness establishes nothing more than that you are perfectly normal.

One good thing about the tension you may feel is that, if not carried to extremes, it can actually be a help rather than a hindrance.

This is so because nervousness keys you up, makes you a bit hyper. This can add a certain vitality and energy to your speaking. Again, nervousness in public performance is not some dreadful aberration peculiar to you alone. It is a perfectly *normal* reaction. Everybody feels it, even the bravest of men. Mohammed Ali, Joe Louis, Jack Dempsey, Sugar Ray Robinson—the greatest prizefighters are nervous when they first walk into the ring and face the crowd. Indeed, their apprehension is directed more toward the audience than toward the opponent.

If you've had any experience with formal relaxation techniques —yoga, transcendental meditation, or anything of the sort—you can employ such means to achieve a more relaxed state as you wait on the speaker's platform to be introduced. But even if you have not had training in such disciplines, you can—believe it or not— calm your nerves to a degree.

First of all, simply *instruct* yourself to relax. This, naturally, is done silently, though your eyes may be either closed or open.

Second, take advantage of knowledge that has long been available to Orientals and is becoming better known in our part of the world—that the act of breathing itself can be employed as an aid to greater relaxation. Michael Keifer, who writes the Sports Clinic column for *Esquire,* has said, "If anxiety is fear of losing control, and breathing is an involuntary reflex that can be put on voluntary override, then perhaps consciously taking control of breathing brings a sense of overall control." I am so confident on this point that I would have deleted the word *perhaps* from Keifer's observation. The very act of deep breathing forces the muscles to a bit of extra exercise and relaxation. It also increases the flow of oxygen to the brain cells and can lower the pulse rate.

Next realize that even if you're not as electrifying a speaker as Jack Kennedy or William F. Buckley you're still probably better at it than anyone in the audience; otherwise one of them would be at the lectern.

Some people tremble when they're nervous. Others do not. If you have the shaky hands problem there are two things to look out for: trying to drink a glass of water and holding your papers close to the microphone. As for the former, no audience wants to see whitecaps in your glass, so if your mouth gets so dry that you absolutely must drink, turn your body around slightly, take one quick swig, and put the glass back down.

The physical reason that a speaker's mouth becomes dry, incidentally, is that in preparing itself for a public performance, the body pumps up extra supplies of adrenaline. This makes the heart beat faster and, in fact, itself contributes somewhat to the feeling of nervousness. But the chemical does give you extra temporary energy and quickens your responses. The slight inhibition of the normal saliva flow is a side effect.

As for your papers, they should be left on the top of the lectern. However, if your eyesight requires that they be held closer to you, beware of permitting them to rattle close to the microphone, since the sound—obviously—will be magnified and your nervousness will become a distraction.

Be comforted by the knowledge that no speaker ever trembled all through a lengthy address. The shaky period usually lasts for just a few minutes, if that, at the beginning of your speech. After your first three or four public addresses it's unlikely to happen at all.

Here is a helpful thought. Think back over all the years of your life. Now focus in on the few occasions when you've heard others speak in public. Can you, at this moment, recall a single instance when you really noticed a speaker's nervousness?

Almost certainly not. The reason is that even if you might have seen a nervous speaker or two, the matter was of such slight importance to you that it made no lasting impression. Keep that in mind when you're on the platform. Even if you are uncomfortable, even if your voice cracks once or twice and your hands tremble, few present will notice—and no one in the audience really gives much of a damn, to tell the truth. You would have to turn pale, pass out, and fall into the orchestra pit before anyone would remember the incident a week later.

Helpful tip: Avoid caffeine. Unless I am overtired I generally will drink no more than half a cup of coffee if I am scheduled to speak at the close of a dinner program. The reason is that extra adrenaline is already flowing when you're getting ready to perform and the addition of a jolt of caffeine can sometimes make you jumpy for purely chemical reasons, even if you weren't before. Although I'm not the nervous type, I once had what was, for me, a strong case of stage fright every night for a week while performing at a Las Vegas nightclub. I finally figured out the reason. Because I was tired from overwork at the time, I had gotten into the habit of drinking one or two Cokes or Pepsis before going on stage, for extra energy. It was the caffeine that was making me nervous, not my professional assignment. I switched to no-caffeine beverages—orange soda, root beer, etc.—and the problem vanished.

I also strongly recommend that you do not try to "solve" the problem of nervous tension by taking tranquilizing medication before you speak. Oh, you'll be more relaxed, all right. But you're also likely to be a bit muddleheaded, have considerably less energy when speaking, and be less acutely tuned in to the reactions of your audience. Ask yourself, as a member of an audience, which kind of speaker you would prefer to listen to—one who is vital and energetic or one who is utterly calm and tranquil?

One of the nice things about problems is that a good many of them do not exist except in our imaginations. Many would-be speakers, for example, fear that since they have already identified themselves—let us assume correctly—as socially shy, they are therefore disqualified by nature from speaking in public. Fortunately, this is not at all the case—something I know from personal experience, since I tend toward shyness, particularly in the presence of strangers in small social gatherings. Nor am I the only public figure who could be so described. Johnny Carson, Dick Cavett, Jack Paar—to mention only a few—are all essentially introverted. Like stutterers who have no trouble singing, we shy introverts often blossom when placed on a stage, in front of a camera, or next to a microphone. So whether you personally are a life-of-the-party type or are inclined to sit and listen to others means little so far as your interest in public speaking is concerned.

Speaking of the nervousness that troubled him during the early part of his TV career, talk-show host Dick Cavett has said, "It varies from night to night. The best thing to do is to tell yourself it doesn't show one-eighth as much as you feel. If you're a little nervous, you don't look nervous at all. If you're very nervous, you look slightly nervous. And if you're totally out of control you look troubled. It scales down on the screen. Anybody who appears on a talk show should always remind himself that everything he's doing looks better than it feels. . . . Your nervous system may be giving you a thousand shocks, but the viewer can only see a few of them."

Nature is never so unfair as when distributing her gifts. Very often there is a true naturalness to superior ability. A great athlete, the best actors or actresses, the musical performers of genius, the great brain surgeons—each is a success partly because the roll of the genetic dice has rewarded him or her with the innate potential for achievement. Such individuals must naturally devote years of hard work to the development of their innate abilities, but it is the gift itself that comes first. Without it, in my opinion, true greatness is rarely achieved.

A perfectly acceptable degree of professional expertise can be reached, nevertheless, even in the absence of such innate genius. A book of instruction such as this cannot have any effect on genetic factors, since those are determined at the moment of conception. The great natural speakers do not require such aids. But the rest of us can profit by a detailed outline of instruction.

You are fortunate, in one respect, that you have chosen to improve your ability in the art of public speaking, rather than, for instance, the art of football playing, acrobatics, acting, dancing, or singing. In all those fields you would be in competition with thousands of able and sometimes quite gifted practitioners. In the field of public speaking, however, there is surprisingly little competition. Most of those called upon to address their peers are, in fact, woefully inept. The only reason they are not hooted away from podiums is that American audiences have become accustomed to the general inadequacy of public speakers. Expectations are now so low that almost any well-intentioned bumbler is, at the very least, accepted— provided he does not drone on for too many minutes.

This means that if you are successful in improving your speaking ability to a marked extent, audiences will not only be relieved but positively grateful at the development of your prowess. So again, be of good cheer. Most people are such poor speakers that even if you are, too, you'll still be treated courteously, which might not be the case if you were an inept pianist, actor, or tap dancer. This is because in the traditional theatrical crafts an extended period of training and experience is considered necessary before one takes to the public stage. As regards public speaking, however, one often just has to start doing it, qualified or not, simply because one has been elected presiding officer of a local Kiwanis Club, made vice-president of a bank, become a leader of a local fund-raising drive, or decided to run for dogcatcher.

There are some people who are perfectly prepared to lecture or perform as long as they are the whole show, but who have a problem if they suspect—or become aware—that another present speaker is much better at the game. What can you do about such a concern if you have it? Well, you might go into fourteen years of psycho-analysis, but I suppose that sort of counsel is impractical. Better advice is to just knock it off. The problem exists entirely in your own mind, not in any sort of objective reality. I've been doing comedy now for about forty years, and I assure you that there have been many occasions during those four decades when on a given show I was not absolutely the funniest person present.

Consider the old "Man-on-the-Street," a brilliant weekly TV comedy sketch that featured Louis Nye, Don Knotts, and Tom Poston. Some nights Louie had the funniest material, other nights Don got the biggest laughs, and on other occasions the honors went to Tom. But never once over the years did anyone say to me, "Boy, I really liked 'Man-on-the-Street' last night, largely because Louis Nye was so much funnier than Tom or Don." Nothing of the kind has ever been said, or even thought.

So if you're part of a large program the best thing that could happen to you is that everybody else does an excellent job. Believe me, no one is going to single you out for special attention. If the whole evening is lively and enjoyable, you'll get your share of the credit. And even if you're the worst of all the speakers, nobody in the audience will care very much—believe it or not.

Don't even be discouraged, by the way, if you have one form of speech impediment or another. Demosthenes, the ancient Greek orator, was troubled by stuttering. He reportedly solved the problem by practicing speaking on the beach with pebbles in his mouth. As a young man, Winston Churchill stammered and even had a slight lisp. Determined to surmount his difficulties, he practiced speaking intensively and eventually became one of the most effective orators of all time. Television host Jack Paar was an early stutterer, too, but largely overcame the problem and went on to become a successful speaker and entertainer.

One question you will have to deal with—because it relates to the problem of nervousness—is whether you should meet the audience, as individuals or en masse, before you speak. There is no rule about this. Do whatever is convenient and comfortable for you.

In situations where I am going to entertain, I usually arrange not to be seen before the moment of my introduction. Such modest glamour as a television performer can project is best concentrated on the moment of appearance. If you're sitting in full view for two hours before you walk on stage, a bit of that mystique wears off. On the other hand, if I'm going to lecture—in either a serious or a humorous vein—I generally prefer to be part of the group before being introduced, since the raw material of the situation—whatever actually happens during the earlier portions of the program, the serving of the lunch or dinner—will usually provide material for jokes or philosophical observations.

On one occasion, for example, I addressed an audience of middle- and upper-class people in the charming community of Santa Barbara, California. During the serving of the meal I noticed that the average age of the audience was about seventy. Later, when someone asked, "What can our nation do about birth control?" I was able to say, "I don't think this particular audience need be unduly concerned with that problem."

If you are a blurt-it-all-out type, it may occur to you that you ought to let the audience know that you're nervous. I recommend against it. A comedian can do it, for his own unique purposes, but others ought to just get down to work and concentrate on the subject matter, not on self. Since the audience, too, ought to be attending to the subject matter, you should not deliberately distract them by making them think of you.

Naturally they'll be reacting to your physical self, but after the speech you certainly won't want them to recall nothing but your nervousness, your hairdo, your attire, and your eyeglasses. You'll want them to recall what you said.

In time, then, and with experience—believe it or not—you will come to feel so at ease on stage that you will be able at one and the same time not only to perform the act of speaking but, with another part of your mind, to monitor your performance as it takes place and make whatever adjustments the situation seems to call for. Not only can your mind do two things at once, it can do many things at once. In fact, it has done so every day of your life since you were born. Think back, for example, to your experience, probably as a teenager, of learning to drive a car. The first two or three times you were all thumbs, concentrating fiercely on what to do with the ignition key, the steering wheel, the brake pedal, the accelerator. Now jump to the present, when it will be common for you to pay almost no conscious attention whatever to the act of driving, but to devote your consciousness to a conversation with a fellow passenger, the content of a radio program, daydreaming, or—in my case—dictating a great deal of business or creative material. Don't be impatient about reaching this phase of relative detachment as a speaker. There's no way it can be rushed. I simply want you to be comforted by the knowledge that such a happy outcome awaits you somewhere ahead on the road of time.

Chapter 2

Writing the Speech

Determining the Subject of Your Speech

Before you put a word on paper you will naturally have to decide, however hazily, just what the general thrust of your speech will be. It is impossible to speak about nothing whatever. Even if you attempted to mouth a disconnected series of words in random order you would still be conveying some combination of impressions. Not to belabor the obvious, you will, then, be speaking about something in particular. That something may grow out of personal experience. You may relate a funny incident you have witnessed, tell a hair-raising story of your experiences during a war, recall your narrow escape from personal disaster, or explain your method of achieving success in a given field.

You may even lecture on a subject with which you have no personal connection whatever other than your interest in it. You might, for example, speak on the death penalty, even though you are unlikely personally to suffer it and have no connection with the law or the prison system. You speak, in such instances, in the capacity of concerned citizen. In this case your remarks will presumably consist partly of factual information gathered in your research and reading, and partly of philosophical observations or recommendations that have occurred to you on the basis of your study and reflection. Your remarks should, of course, reflect much more than your personal bias.

Know the Subject

As a young man I was in favor of the death penalty, although I had never thought the matter through in any detailed way. I did view the reality of capital punishment as tragic, but I simply assumed that it was necessary for the protection of society. Some years later I became interested enough in the subject to begin to read about it, at which point I made a startling discovery: I was literally unable to find a single book in *favor* of capital punishment. This in itself made a powerful impression on me, because it obviously meant that scholars who had taken the trouble to do the great volume of research required in writing a nonfiction book had all come to the same conclusion: that the death penalty was nothing more than institutionalized revenge, a holdover from an earlier and harsher stage in the development of civilization.

You don't have to agree with me on this point, needless to say. I introduce it here only by way of suggesting that if you plan to lecture on any subject that is the least bit complex or controversial you should approach it with as open a mind as possible and do a good bit of study before you publicly address yourself to the question. If you do so, even if you persist in your present opinions, you will defend them more ably, and—who knows?—a disinterested study of the facts may incline you to change your views, whatever they might be, on whatever subject.

Focus the Speech

Your purpose in lecturing may be to instruct—to tell an audience something about a scholarly subject, to explain how to repair an automobile engine or how to reduce utility bills.

The primary reason that it is necessary to bring your subject into focus for yourself at the outset is that doing so will make it easier to come to certain later decisions. It will, for example, suggest to you the proper method and tone with which to address your audiences. A talk about the technique of planting roses, for instance, will hardly be delivered in the same tone and with the same manner that it would be reasonable to employ in exhorting your listeners to action in the context of some pressing or outrageous social problem.

Even the speed with which you speak will be, in part, determined by the nature of your subject. If the message you are conveying is technical and complex, you should write your speech as clearly and simply as possible. When you deliver it, you should speak slowly, enunciate well, repeat certain fundamental points, and use no terms unfamiliar to your listeners without defining them. If, on the other hand, you are giving a talk about one of last Saturday's football games, both your style and your delivery can be quick, light, and bantering.

A clear definition of your subject matter will also tell you whether it makes sense to employ the device of humor. It is not necessary that your subject be essentially trivial to open with a few jokes. On the other hand, there are situations where humor is inappropriate. This will almost invariably be the case if you are delivering remarks at a memorial service or on a patriotic or other solemn occasion.

Establishing the Purpose of Your Speech

Purpose vs. Title

Once you know the subject of your speech, you can determine the purpose of it—and, incidentally, its title. It is by no means necessary to have an actual title before you begin to write. We may be sure that at the top of the envelope on which he wrote his now-famous speech, Abraham Lincoln did not write the words *The Gettysburg Address*. The title of your own address usually emerges quite naturally from the text itself. Again, it is not even necessary that your remarks have a title. Speech titles are almost never announced to audiences, although they are sometimes included in printed programs or promotional literature. So don't spend more than ten seconds bothering about the title. Titles, as such, are almost never good or bad; they're just functional.

What matters is the purpose of your speech. This will not have to be announced to an audience, either, but establishing it will help to clarify your own thinking. An expression of purpose will usually begin with the word *to*. To explain the effects of natural radiation. To urge campaign workers to increase their efforts. To convert others to your form of Christianity. To encourage support of your school's football team. To convince your audience that there is too much violence on television. It is essential to have your own purpose clearly in mind, since this will tend to concentrate your thinking on the point or issue.

The title of your speech concerns a topic; the purpose of it expresses your objective. The topic may be Ping-Pong, the latest Republican Party platform, or the use of addictive drugs. Your purpose will be either to provide general information about the topic or to press for a particular point of view on it.

A title may, of course, also express your point of view: "Why the Use of Cocaine Must Never Be Legalized," "Why the Death Penalty Is Not an Effective Deterrent," "Why Christians Should Not Be Members of the Ku Klux Klan," and so on.

There is one context, however, in which a title will be necessary. If you are addressing a formal conference, in which you may be one of many speakers, the delivery of your speech will be considered "giving a paper." Titles are required.

The Seventh Annual Conference of the Western Society of Criminology, for example, took as its 1980 theme *Crime and Justice in the Eighties*. Separate panel sessions had specific titles such as "Police Strikes and the Unionization Movement," "The Future of Probation and Parole," "Law Enforcement in the Eighties," "Crime and Delinquency Research," and so on.

Individual addresses under such titles have their own titles. The panel session "Alternatives to the Justice System" involved the delivery of addresses titled "Developing Criteria for Alternatives to Incarceration," "Competing Models of Criminal Justice," "Alternatives to Incarceration: The Cuban Experience," "Research in Juvenile Justice Decision Making: An Absence of Criminological Imagination," and "Community Alternatives to Incarceration—the Role of Public and Private Agencies in Expertise."

Purpose and Persuasion

Quite early in the history of rhetoric, scholars discerned that there were four basic kinds of communication or discourse.

1. *Exposition* is used when you wish to inform your audience, to deliver factual information to them.
2. *Argument* is used to affect the opinions of your listeners.
3. *Description* is used to give the listeners a more or less visual impression of something, to make them see it in their minds.
4. *Narration* is used when you want your audience to follow the movement of a story.

This is all obvious enough, but reality has a way of being more ambiguous and confusing than theory. It will rarely be the case, therefore, that you will limit yourself to just one of these kinds of discourse. You may, in fact, employ all of them in one address. The important thing is to be clear in your own mind as to just which methods you are employing, at what times, and for what purposes.

Some experts on the subject of public speaking feel that it is an absolute requirement that your public remarks include a persuasive element. They recommend that you take a clear-cut position on whatever it is you're talking about and work to bring the audience to your point of view.

Art Linkletter, for example, has written:

Under no circumstances should you omit this last opinion-forming stage in your preparation! It's absolutely essential that, in effect, a speaker have a definite position—a clear-cut set of convictions on what he's talking about. If you don't believe in what you're saying, you can't be a truly effective public speaker.

Well, as it happens, it is *not* "absolutely essential" that every speech be an exercise in persuasive rhetoric. It's perfectly possible to give a talk that is simply instructive. You might discuss the water system of the Pacific Northwest, outline a history of the Iroquois Indians, or deal with a thousand and one other subjects with no intention of doing more than sharing information. Obviously you're perfectly at liberty (in the United States, anyway) to let an audience know that you are for or against capital punishment, gun control, forest preservation, or whatever; my point is that this—Art Linkletter and others to the contrary—is not an essential requirement.

Organizing Your Remarks

The Opening

It is at the writing stage that you begin to decide not only what you will say but also what you will do. Some speakers prefer to get right to work in addressing an audience, without attempting any particularly dramatic or unusual introduction. Others feel that an opening attention-getter is helpful, if not essential. There's no right or wrong on the point; make your own decisions, or try one approach in a certain instance and another on a second occasion.

On the opening day of a biology class during my freshman year at Drake University in Des Moines, Iowa, the first thing the instructor did was to pick up what turned out to be a hard-boiled egg and toss it to me. Reflexively, I caught it, at which point the professor launched into a discussion of the classification of living creatures that lay eggs. The attention of the class, of course, was immediately riveted on the subject and we were off and running.

I don't suggest that you begin all your lectures by tossing an egg out to the audience, even if you're speaking on biology. You'll be lucky, perhaps, if the audience doesn't toss eggs at you. Some speakers use a statistic to capture the attention of an audience. For example,

> More children under the age of five die from injuries inflicted by their parents than from tuberculosis, polio, diabetes, rheumatic fever, and appendicitis combined.

Needless to say, if you employ statistics—either as attention-getting devices or to support your arguments—do not be guilty of Ronald Reaganism. As his warmest admirers were often aware, during his campaigns for the presidency Reagan repeatedly was careless with statistics, and consequently sometimes gave a distorted picture of the situations to which he was referring. His advisers, fortunately, quickly remedied such errors. But a statistic that you have checked out—especially if it carries information that will come as a surprise or shock to your audience—can serve very well as an attention-getting device.

If you decide to open with a joke, be certain that the story has some relevance to the occasion. Few things are more embarrassing than hearing a speaker tell the old-fashioned "Two Jews got off a streetcar" or "A priest, a minister, and a rabbi were out in a rowboat" type of story, adding a comment such as "Well, so much for that!" and then clumsily getting around to the business of the moment.

So use an opening "gimmick" only if it's your natural style. You're under no obligation either way.

A word of caution: It's better not to try something too bizarre and have it fail. With a more conventional introduction you're less likely to get into trouble.

Whatever your introduction, the primary rule is to keep it short. This is so even if you've been granted a full hour for your lecture. And if you're only permitted a few minutes it's not wise to waste three or four of them ingratiating yourself.

Conventional opening remarks often have nothing whatever to do with the body of your address. They may involve an expression of thanks to the person who introduced you, particularly if the introduction consisted in part of compliments. Or, if the introduction is brief, factual, and totally uncomplimentary, you may want to make capital of the fact. A speaker once introduced me by saying, "And now, ladies and gentlemen, Steve Allen." I was able to turn his abruptness to my advantage by saying, "—and I'd like to thank your chairman for that very flattering introduction."

In most cases, however, you need not try to be funny but should simply acknowledge the chairman, distinguished guests, if any, and the "ladies and gentlemen" who constitute the audience.

As regards especially important guests, by the way, you may have to be selective if you're speaking at one of those "all-the-trimmings" functions graced by a dais at which perhaps a dozen or more notables may be seated. In that case you should not attempt to name them all, since it finally comes to sound somewhat comic if you go on saying, "Thank you, Mr. Chairman, Mayor Bradley, Governor Harris, Senator Thompson, Robert Redford, Monsignor O'Brien, Donald Duck, etc., etc." Select just a name or two or three and then add a phrase such as "and other distinguished guests."

If you're still not sure how to handle this detail, then pay careful attention the next time you're in an audience at such an event and a speaker is introduced. It's really quite simple and therefore need give you no serious cause for concern.

The Middle

The bulk of your preparatory work—at the writing stage—will of course be on the main body of your speech itself. Don't worry about not having enough ideas. In almost every case, speakers have the opposite problem. They have so many points they want to make that it is usually not possible for them to do so within the imposed time limits.

Speaking of time limits, never leave yourself in the slightest doubt as to how long you will be expected to speak. If you can't figure it out, then ask. Sometimes the organizers of public functions are reluctant to tell a speaker that he or she is allotted only a brief time. You may, therefore, have to pry the information out of them. But pry away, because it's in your interest to do so. Many initially successful speeches have ended up failures simply because, instead of concluding at the appropriate moment, they went on and on.

This middle or main portion of your address, obviously, constitutes the general statement of your case. It need not have any apparently logical structure, although there is nothing wrong with such a formulation. Just making your basic points and hammering them home will suffice.

If you have had a high school or college education you may have acquired the impression that it is necessary to prepare a formal outline prior to writing almost anything. It's not so. This is not to say that outlines are not helpful. They can be useful in providing a skeletal form according to which you can organize your general observations. But doing so is no more necessary in the case of a speech than in the context of any other literary endeavor.

I never use an outline but prefer a numerical listing of the points I wish to bring out. The points as they are later developed can be written or typed without being numbered, but you may find the numbers helpful as an eye aid on the platform even if you do not refer to them aloud.

The Third Part

What remains is, of course, the conclusion. Some lecturers devote great attention to developing a flashy, dramatic finish, and there's nothing wrong with that approach at all. Most speakers, however, do not attach that much importance to concluding their talks. Depending on the nature of your speech, it may be appropriate to review quickly—just as a memory refresher—four or five of the main points you've made. If you've taken up most of your time making them, however, and have only a minute or so in which to close, the "let-me-list-again-for-you" approach will not be possible.

In that case, simply restate the importance or significance of the argument you've been making, and—if doing so is appropriate—solicit the involvement or assistance of your audience. If, for example, you gave a speech about the problem of littering, you might wish to close by saying something like the following:

> In closing, ladies and gentlemen, I'll observe that it is all very easy to criticize. In fact, most of us are quite gifted at that. But criticism alone has never solved a single problem.

Criticism is necessary, but it is effective only if it moves us to action. So in addition to trying to cut down littering by others—for example, all those thoughtless slobs we see throwing cigarettes, beer cans, and wastepaper out of car windows—let's make sure that we ourselves are not guilty of such offenses.

In many situations it will also be appropriate, at the close, to devote just a few seconds to thanking the host organization for having invited you to give your talk, and to share your thanks, too, with the ladies and gentlemen who have just listened to you. If there has been a question-and-answer period, you may want to direct a remark or two to some who posed questions:

"And my thanks go to Mrs. Fuller, here in the front row, who was kind enough to raise the question of what we might expect the City Council to do to assist in this campaign."

Composing the Speech

Ask yourself at the outset, "How good am I at writing anything?" Obviously, if you've always had difficulty writing essays, term papers, or short stories, you may also find it heavy going when you try to write a speech.

Do not despair. A speech is considerably easier to write, since you can even get away with certain errors—of spelling, punctuation, sentence structure, logic—that would stand out noticeably on the typed or printed page. That doesn't mean you can write any kind of nonsense and expect it to be well received, but it should reduce your sense of being under pressure to know that the requirements for preparing an effective speech are less rigorous than those involved in learning the proper methods of English composition. The reason is that when your words are committed to print they are subject to leisurely and repeated scrutiny. Any errors, therefore, are likely to be detected. A speech, on the other hand, is over and done with in a single instance.

There are cases, of course, of public figures who, year after year, continue to use essentially the same speech. One prominent political

figure, over a period of almost twenty years, recited the same speech
so effectively that eventually he became elected to high office largely
on its merits. Even in such cases, though, the address is not likely
to be heard twice by any one audience. Therefore, most errors will
probably pass unnoticed.

I once heard quite a forceful address delivered by a prominent
writer of screenplays. So impressed was I, in fact, by his comments
that when I saw he had discarded the typed version of his remarks
I picked it up and gave it a few moments' study. I was greatly
surprised to discover that the talk was not nearly as well written,
nor the arguments as well reasoned, as I had assumed.

Some speakers have such warm, natural charm that they can
sell almost any sort of message and make almost any address seem
weighty or profound. A classic instance was Sir Laurence Olivier's
remarks at the 1979 Academy Awards ceremony. Millions of television viewers across the country were deeply impressed by the
dignity and charm of Olivier's gracious comments. The next day,
however, those who studied the published transcript of his brief talk
were surprised to discover that there really wasn't a great deal of
substance to it. What had gripped the audience was the total impression: the noble face—still handsome in old age—the rich, genteel
voice, the dignity and bearing of an English gentleman, and the
natural talent of a consummate actor. If you are similarly blessed,
more power to you. But if not, you'll be well advised to write or
plan your remarks with great care.

Generating Ideas

One of my "secrets" for doing creative work of any sort is simply
to do what I call "getting out of my own way."

I discovered, quite early in life, that there is some strange creative
center in my brain that, once stimulated, will give up a considerable
volume of whatever I ask it to produce: jokes, stories, philosophical
observations, or ideas for essays, newspaper or magazine features,
television comedy sketches, plays, songs, and so on. Part of the
process involves shutting "me" up, calming myself down, relaxing,
and just listening to the ideas as an internal computer cranks them
out.

I know it's all very easy for someone who has written a good many books, songs, plays, or whatever to suggest that you, too, can do likewise, and with equal ease. I'm saying no such thing. After all, I can't write a play as well as Neil Simon, a melody as well as Jerome Kern, a lyric as well as Stephen Sondheim, or a short story as well as John Cheever. But that's a point of no importance whatever. So don't worry if, when you first begin timidly listening to your own creative center, it doesn't immediately begin cranking out ideas that would dazzle Aristotle.

By simply agreeing to give a speech, or by self-generating a plan to do so, you will have stimulated your own mysterious idea center. What you must do next is *listen to its responses.* At this stage don't— whatever you do—serve as a censorious judge, telling yourself, "Oh, that's no good" or "That will never work." Stopping self-criticism at once is part of the process of getting out of your own way.

Whatever thoughts occur to you, make an immediate note of them. It is assumed, of course, that you will have the common sense to keep yourself provided with pencil and paper or a small portable tape recorder. Then, by whatever means, grab any and every relevant idea that occurs to you. You may make your notations on separate slips of paper or on cards, or list them on one piece of paper. Some speakers prefer yellow lined legal pads for this purpose. On the left-hand side of the page enumerate the points as you make them. Then, over to the right, revise the order in any way that seems reasonable.

In her autobiography Margaret Sanger refers to such a method employed by Havelock Ellis in preparing his books and articles.

If when traveling . . . on the tram, going to a concert, shopping . . . outside the [British] Museum, a thought came to him, he would pull out a bit of paper and jot down notes. That was how he compiled his material for books, gathering it piecemeal and storing it away in envelopes. Anything on the Dance went into the Dance envelope, Music into Music, and so on.

As soon as any one became full enough to attract his attention, he took it out and started to make something out of it.

Now determine from your list or cards which points are the most important. Then either eliminate the least meaningful ones or include them only by way of a quick, passing reference, thus permitting yourself more time to develop the essential elements of your presentation.

Suppose that by this notation process you produce thirty separate ideas relating to the subject of your speech. As you review them you might decide that five or six points simply aren't suitable for your purposes. Who cares? You've still got all the others. And that's only from the first day's pickings. Assuming that you don't have to give your talk immediately, you'll probably have quite a few days—perhaps weeks—to listen to your internal creative center. If you're at all normal, you will almost certainly come up with not too few ideas, but too many.

Researching a Topic

After selecting a topic and collecting ideas you may realize that your general purpose requires more support than your combined memory and imagination can supply. In this case you will have to do research, a fancy word for looking things up in books. An important advantage of such study is that it enables you to stud your remarks with specifics. Unless you are a scholar, you will probably get all the information you need from books, newspapers, and magazines. The place to find such resources is, of course, a library. Bookstores are also stocked with useful reference works, but buying books is a good deal more expensive than borrowing them.

In my own case, I rarely find it necessary to refer to public libraries, because I have an enormous collection of books that fills probably far too many shelves in several rooms. One room in particular houses about fifteen hundred three-ringed loose-leaf notebooks in which are filed significant articles I've read on various important subjects over the past thirty years. I am, fortunately, able to read at a fast rate, but I also underline and make marginal notes when studying material to which I might want to refer in the future. The underlines enable me to find the meat of the article quickly when I consult it a second time.

Although my note taking—in fact, all my writing—is done by

speaking into a small, hand-held tape recorder, you may find this method unsuitable. It would not work for me, either, were it not that I am fortunate enough to have a staff of secretaries who do the necessary transcribing and typing. On the rare occasions when I do visit a library, I dictate notes—in as soft a voice as possible, of course. It's more convenient than writing longhand, since we can all speak faster than we can write.

Since you will probably be writing your notes, you should decide whether you wish to use small three-by-five note cards or notebooks. Cards have the advantage that their order can be changed as often as suits your purposes.

Remember that it is ordinarily not necessary to do an enormous volume of research when all you are preparing for is the writing of a speech that may take no more than twenty minutes to deliver. Authors planning to write a book that may run to four hundred pages naturally have to devote a great deal more time to the task.

Another source of information is the sort of work that private detectives do: personal investigation. If you are writing a speech on prison reform, for instance, you might visit a prison or two, interview officials of the institutions, and talk to prisoners or to ex-convicts.

You may also choose to conduct your own survey or poll, putting questions about your subject to a certain number of people and tabulating the results.

Writing the Speech

"Be yourself," at the typewriter as well as at the lectern. If your normal style of speech and writing is simple and direct, don't suddenly try to write like Thomas Jefferson. Don't make the error common to speakers such as Spiro Agnew or William F. Buckley, the too-many-big-words problem. In Agnew's case he was not particularly erudite and therefore came across as a show-off when he used polysyllabic words he had probably learned from *Reader's Digest's* "It Pays to Increase Your Word Power." In the case of Bill Buckley, he is literate, an intellectual, so his personal vocabulary is legitimately rich. But one sometimes has the impression that the audience or readership to whom he is truly appealing is not the one that is listening to him or reading him at the moment, but some invisible company of scholars or critics of a future time. In the interest of addressing such august company, he will occasionally leave his actual hearers or readers in the dark—which, sometimes, is perhaps just as well.

Don't try to compose your speech in a hurry. It will be better if you do not attempt to write it all at once. Give yourself some time, not only to do research, but to clarify your own thinking.

Some speechwriters simply roll up their sleeves and get started on the job of composition, just as they would if writing a letter to a relative. Again, others prefer to construct an outline first, or a list of points.

There is no right or wrong about the matter. In my own case I just start writing, as separate ideas occur to me, though they never come in any simple beginning-to-end order.

It may be the case that this evening you will start to write a speech of approximately twenty pages, but that, after the completion of just a few hundred words, you have nothing more to say on the subject for the moment. No problem; simply set the project aside and get back to it later.

After you have completed a first draft, you may then make additional decisions as to which portions go in which positions. Something originally conceived as part of the conclusion, for example, might turn out to be more suitable for the opening.

Editing the Speech

My first instruction on editing is to buy a book called *The Elements of Style*, by William Strunk, Jr. This moderately famous volume, long endorsed by that graceful practitioner of the prose arts, E.B. White, is short, precise, and wonderfully helpful as regards any and all forms of writing. It is a mistake, of course, to read important books only once. *The Elements of Style* should remain on your desk or bedside table for the rest of your life, as important a part of your personal library as a dictionary. It can teach you not only to write better but to function as an editor.

Successful professional authors or journalists learn—usually quite early—to serve as their own editors. They are also fortunate enough to have their own copy scrutinized by professional editors, who specialize in that task, so that by publication time mistakes of style, spelling, grammar, and punctuation are cut to a minimum. Since, however, you are unlikely to have available to you the services of a professional editor, you will have to perform this function yourself.

Get a firm grasp on the fact that it is far better to be a harsh critic at the stage when no one but yourself has seen your speech. Failure on this point can mean that you will eventually be subject to the judgments of the several hundred editors comprising your audience, some or all of whom may be more sensitive to your errors than you were yourself.

All professional writers learn—sometimes, at first, with much discomfort—that their first drafts are practically never suitable as is. Important speeches, such as those delivered by American presidents, may go through as many as a dozen drafts before delivery. I have never forgotten how instructive was the moment, early in the 1950s, when I happened to see the manuscript of a best-selling novel by James Jones displayed in the window of a Fifth Avenue bookstore. Several pages were fanned open, and I was surprised to note the many editorial corrections, deletions, arrows, and other scribbles on every visible page.

If presidents and best-selling novelists edit their material to such a degree, or have it edited by others, you might as well go along with the practice.

For psychological reasons it's not necessary to delve into here, it is notoriously difficult to edit your own material shortly after you've written it. Certainly you can start the process then, but the ego is generally plugged into the creation so firmly at that point that you'll find it painful to make deletions or other improvements. Set the material aside for a few days, therefore, so that you can consciously forget it. You'll be surprised by how many errors, typographical and otherwise, you can find when you look at it again.

I have deliberately avoided in this chapter giving examples that, simply because of the wide variety of human occupations and interests, will almost certainly be of interest to only a small percentage of this book's readers. Some manuals on the art of public speaking devote long paragraphs to explaining, for example, that if surgeons speak to laymen they must not make the error of using obscure medical terms for diseases, parts of the body, or surgical techniques. The point is perfectly sound and, in my opinion, requires no further extrapolation. I see no reason for writing an extended example of such a talk. One text I've seen, which is in other respects quite helpful, devotes sixteen paragraphs to a sample outline on the subject of baseball. The fact is, however, that the number of public lecturers who will speak on that subject constitutes a fraction of 1 percent. Since I assume that everyone intelligent enough to read a book such as this will at least have had a pass at outlining in high school, there's no point in showing you again how to do something you learned when you were fifteen years old.

Typing the Speech

If you are an inept typist and do not have a secretary, then you'll have to have somebody else do the job for you—a friend, family member, or hired temporary worker. Abraham Lincoln, a naturally gifted orator, was able to work with a few notes on the back of an envelope—at Gettysburg, at least—but, trust me, in the twentieth century it's wise to take advantage of the technology available.

In typing your speech—or having it done for you if you are a klutz at the keyboard—keep in mind that you're going to have to *read* the copy in circumstances that are unlikely to be ideal for reading. There is the possibility that a strong spotlight—perhaps more than one—will be shining into your eyes. The pupil of the eye automatically contracts to prevent pain and injury. But if your eyes are adjusting to a glaring spotlight you may find it difficult to see papers a couple of feet below eye level, even if there is a small lectern light shining on them.

There are typewriters that can print in a size larger than that usually seen in letters. A few minutes of experimenting at home can tell you if you need that kind of aid. If you do—and don't get it—you can be in trouble.

Typing important thoughts into separate paragraphs is also a convenient eye aid on the platform. Anyone intelligent enough to write a personal letter has no difficulty knowing when to start a new paragraph. But in having your speech typed I suggest that you specify even more paragraph headings—with indentations—than if you were preparing an essay for publication.

Needless to say, you *never* try to read a speech that is single-spaced, because you'll almost certainly get lost the first time you look away from the page and out to the audience. Double-spacing is the norm; some speakers even prefer to have material triple-spaced, which makes it even easier for the eye to follow the text, particularly when reading from a standing position.

Those of us whose professional background is in radio use a common page-marking technique that is perfectly suited to the lecture platform. In reading a commercial, a news item, a joke in a comedy script, or a serious line in a dramatic script, we *underline* words that we want to emphasize, and draw a slanted line between words or sentences if we want to make a pause. I sometimes use the inverted *P* mark to indicate paragraphs—like a book or newspaper editor—even though the copy at such a point may already have been indented by the typist. My purpose is to be reminded that a new thought, a new angle of argument or exposition, is being introduced.

Just about the worst thing that can happen to a writer is to spend weeks, months—perhaps years—working on a manuscript and then lose the only existing version of it. Some readers will interpret this to mean that you should keep two copies. But there is no reason to so limit yourself. While you will hardly need forty-seven versions of any important paper, it's a good idea to have three or four. For obvious reasons, these should not all be stored in the same place. In the old days it was sometimes troublesome to make duplicates, but now—with modern photocopying equipment—that's no longer a problem. Be sure that if you make insertions, deletions, or significant additions as the speech develops and evolves, all copies reflect the changes.

Writing with Accuracy and Clarity

Use Words Precisely

In expressing your ideas use words reasonably and with due precision. Try to be as careful with words as scientists are with test tubes, chemicals, and electric currents. The reason is that we do most of our thinking with words. Most of our communicating with other people is done with words, too. Always try, therefore, to use the appropriate word to express your thought.

It's not that words themselves really paint exact pictures of things; as a matter of fact, they don't. They often have a fuzzy or vague meaning rather than a clear, sharp one. Some words have many meanings.

Take the word *mean*, for example.

If you say, "President Lincoln came from a very *mean* background," the definition is "modest or poor." But you might also say, "Jerry, don't be *mean* to Sally."

One might say, "What do you *mean?*" And there are other interpretations of the word. The point is that it's precisely because words are often vague or ambiguous in meaning that you must not only be careful when using them, but tolerant in reasoning with others. The meaning of a word may change depending upon who says it, when he says it, where he says it, and how he says it.

You ought not to react to *words* as you would to the reality that they represent. Some people, for example, have such an emotional reaction to the word *communist* that it actually handicaps them in dealing rationally—even in opposition—with real communists and their activities.

Understand the Difference between Fact and Opinion

A fact—if I'm not getting too basic—is something that is really true. For example: The first president of the United States of America was George Washington. That's a fact. It's a fact from the past. There are also millions of facts we can see about us at present. It's a fact that you are reading this book right now.

But suppose you and a friend are eating banana ice cream cones and someone asks you both, "Does banana ice cream taste good?"

You might say, "Yes!"

And your friend might say, "Yeeeaacchh! No!"

Now, which is fact and which opinion?

Both the "yes" and the "no" are opinions. An opinion merely tells how you feel about something, whether you like it or not. It would be absurd for you and your friend to argue about banana ice cream, because both of you are giving your honest opinion. Nobody is right and nobody is wrong.

It's perfectly all right to have opinions. We all have thousands of them. But don't make the mistake of thinking that your feelings—your likes and dislikes—are the same as facts. Be on guard against saying you *know* something when what you're talking about is not really knowledge but opinion.

Another kind of opinion might be called a wrong fact. For example, it might be your opinion that the state of Florida is just north of California. But it isn't. You simply have an opinion about a question of fact. Your opinion may be right or wrong. The important thing is to remember the difference between facts and opinions in constructing your speech.

Beware of Overstating Your Case

A friend of mine, a very bright person, happens to be correct in perhaps 90 percent of her opinions and observations. But even some of her soundest comments are not properly received because she's careless with the use of the words *never* and *always*. She might, for example, say, "I never smoke," when in fact she may smoke four or five cigarettes a month. Or she will say, "They always act as if they—" when what she means is "They *often* act as if they—"

The reason such words should be used only when they are justified is that by overstating the case you may arouse a resentful or argumentative response. Similarly, avoid exaggeration, unless it's deliberately used for humorous or dramatic effect.

What to Do about the Word I

In the old days it was considered poor form to use the first person singular pronoun at all in certain kinds of writing and extremely poor form to use it a great deal. Such usage seemed to suggest vanity and concentration on self rather than the subject matter. To do so is no longer regarded as offensive as it formerly was, but this does not mean that you can be profligate as regards self-reference. It's sensible to avoid the sometimes awkward alternatives to *I*—"this

speaker" or "we personally feel"—and you have considerably more
latitude when writing a speech then when preparing a formal paper.
Audiences will not only be curious but may insist on knowing how
you personally feel about the issue under discussion.

Using Statistics

Some people assume that dealing with specifics is largely a matter
of citing facts and figures, but this is not the case. You should
employ mathematical references only when they are simple enough
to be understood by everyone in your audience.

I recommend, in this connection, that you read an old book
titled *How to Lie with Statistics* by Darrell Huff. It could—God
forbid—teach you how to be devious by manipulating statistical
information, although one hopes that would not be your purpose.
But the book will help clarify your own thinking about arithmetical
information and percentages and will, if interpreted properly, make
you more responsible in using them.

Huff's book also shows how a statement may be factually true
but nevertheless utterly misleading unless the listener is familiar
with the larger context in which the statistics are based. A statistic,
for example, suggesting that the average American now earns three
times as much money as he did in 1940 will be misleading unless
one appreciates that the U.S. dollar in 1985 was worth only a
fraction of what it was four and a half decades earlier.

You have, of course, the moral obligation to be as honest as
possible in citing factual information of any kind. If you deliberately
distort the record simply to lend support to your argument, then
you are, among other things, a liar. You can become an embarrassed
liar as well, if your deception is perceived while you are on the
platform.

In most cases—God help us—you will, in fact, get away with
such errors and/or lies. Hitler was so confident on the point that
he and his fellow Nazis openly told endless lies on the theory that
a certain percentage of them would be believed, and that if one
colossal lie were told often enough a sizable percentage of the population would eventually come to believe it. But there is more than

enough falsehood and misinformation in the world. Do what you can to diminish, not increase, the amount.

Quoting Authorities

Unless you are qualified by personal experience to speak on your chosen topic (a doctor on medicine, a lawyer on the judicial system, a football coach on athletics), you may be wise to include in your address references to acknowledged authorities. Regarding the question of which authorities to quote, there are two factors to keep in mind. You may refer to individuals of stature on the question at issue, or you may quote people for whom a specific audience has particular respect.

Suppose, for example, that you wish to give a speech on behalf of the United Nations, and have been invited to address an audience comprised largely of Catholics. You would obviously be better advised to quote the Popes, who have repeatedly endorsed the United Nations, than Bertrand Russell.

If you're addressing an audience of political conservatives, quote Barry Goldwater, William F. Buckley, or Ronald Reagan.

If you're addressing a pro-ERA group, quote Susan B. Anthony, Gloria Steinem, or Mary Wollestonecraft.

Beware, however, of quoting too many authorities or of letting any one quotation run on too long.

If the appeal to authority suits your style, you'll be glad to know that much of the basic research has already been done. *Bartlett's Familiar Quotations* is a good source; another is *The Great Quotations* by Gilbert Seldes (Lyle Stuart). You may also clip and save articles from newspapers and magazines for this purpose.

Develop Your Own Powers of Reason

Dependence on authority is, of course, a two-edged sword. For long centuries the intellectual development of Europe was hampered by an overdependence on the views of Aristotle, who—though he may have been the wisest man who ever lived—was nevertheless wrong about a good many things. European scholars of the Middle Ages had such respect for the Greek philosopher that his writings were used much as the Bible is among fundamentalist Christians: to simply end an argument—at least to the satisfaction of the quoter— by reference to any portion of the ancient text which undercuts an opponent's case.

Parenthetically, in some of my speeches on the subject of general semantics I sometimes deliberately trick an audience and then reveal both the deception and its purpose.

I might say, for example, "No less an authority than George Washington has said, 'There can be such a thing as too much freedom of the press.' "

After a moment's pause to permit the audience to reflect on this remarkable assertion, I then explain that to my knowledge Washington never said anything of the sort.

But I ask you to think back now to your reactions of a moment ago when I attributed the observation to so respected a figure from American history. Did you find yourself going along with the point, or at least thinking that perhaps there might be something to it? It's irrelevant to our purposes of the moment whether the assertion is true or untrue, wise or foolish. The purpose of deceiving you was to suggest that we must analyze statements on their own merits and not be so easily inclined to accept or reject them on the basis of our prejudice about the source.

In other instances, in a discussion of the question of how our society might go about solving perplexing social problems, I have said, "Let me give you here two blatant examples of communist propaganda." I then quote two paragraphs which indeed sound consistent with Marxist philosophy, although I subsequently reveal that the author of one of the paragraphs was Pope Pius XII and the author of the other was Abraham Lincoln.

The point, again, is that we ought to use our own rational powers to evaluate what we hear and not be either easily taken in or put off by our feelings about the speaker or writer quoted. But because most people are easily influenced by the views of authority figures they admire, you might as well make judicious use of the ploy.

Far better than dependence on outside authorities will be a well-reasoned argument that applies precisely to the question at issue. To construct such an argument it will be necessary for you to think. There is far more to thinking than simply setting down, in partially random order, a series of observations on the subject matter you have chosen. You will also have to construct a case that is logically consistent. Just as there are those with gifts for music, mathematics, or athletics, so there are those who have special aptitudes for coherent, logical thought. But even those of us without such gifts can, by applying ourselves, reason better than we ordinarily do.

Do not be deluded, incidentally, that all that is needed is a return to good old-fashioned common sense. That there is a shortage of common sense no one would deny. But we need much more. Common sense might be compared to playing a musical instrument by ear. It's nice if you can do it, but it's better if you can also read music and know something about the theory behind it. Common sense for long centuries made people very comfortable in their certainty that the earth was flat, that the sun went around the earth, that the sun and the moon were the same size, and that the sky was blue.

We start—if we are fortunate—with common sense, but to it we must add the applied power of reasoning, aided by the observations and methods of science.

It has always been important for people to think. Those who develop the knack find our world a much less puzzling and frightening place. They understand things better, and consequently are better able to plan and control their activities than are people who think less well.

Today it is more important than ever before to think as clearly as possible. The world we live in is a more difficult place, in some ways, than it ever was before. Our society faces a long list of troublesome problems: what to do about pollution of air and water; how to achieve peace and avoid war; what to do about drug abuse, crime, poverty, disagreements between black and white people, and so on. These and other dilemmas can be solved—if at all—only if we *think clearly* about them.

Some people today are responding to such depressing puzzles

by deliberately turning away from reason and, instead, taking an interest in astrology, fortune-telling, or vague philosophies—collections of ideas—that seem to promise peace and understanding, but which for most people do not really provide concrete solutions to either personal or social problems.

What the world needs now is not only "love, sweet love," but good, straight thinking. As a public speaker you can make a contribution toward that ideal.

Considering Your Audience

There is no such thing as a speech which will be appropriate for any and all audiences. At the writing stage, you must give careful consideration to the makeup of your audience. If you are preparing an address from scratch, you do not have to worry about the fifty-seven variations on it that you might be subsequently delivering to as many separate audiences. But you do have to bear your basic audience in mind. Fortunately this is something you've already been doing your entire life, so it does not call for the exercise of heretofore unimagined gifts.

You are naturally aware that you do not speak to a four-year-old child in the same way you speak to a forty-year-old adult. You do not address your boss with quite the same bantering tone with which you speak to your fellow employees. We speak one way to those we love, another to those we are not especially fond of. We speak in one style to friends and in a somewhat different manner to strangers. The same thing goes for different kinds of audiences.

People who are new to the business of speechwriting—whether the remarks are to be delivered by themselves or by others—often overlook the fact that spoken language differs from written language. A speech is designed not for the eye but for the ear. This may seem both obvious and unimportant. As a matter of fact, it is of enormous importance. The reader, who can set his own pace and can go back to restudy any sentence or paragraph whose meaning may have momentarily eluded him, is quite a different sort of creature from the listener, who has no control whatever over the pace at which a message is delivered to him. That is entirely in the speaker's control. This means that quite a different form of communication is involved. Be aware of the difference.

As a writer of prose you may let your sentences ramble on at considerable length, so long as you do not lose control of them. As a speaker you should keep your sentences relatively short. Never forget that no matter how brilliant and well constructed your formal address is, even the most attentive listener is not going to absorb your entire message. This is a tragedy, but like all tragedies it must be faced, not denied.

Our concentrated attention wanders, literally every few seconds, even when we are attempting to overcome such a natural failing. You can prove this very simply by saying a sentence equivalent in length to two or three lines of printed type, then asking your listener to repeat what has just been said. Not once in a hundred times will you hear the sentence repeated exactly as you spoke it.

C.S. Lewis clarifies the point in the preface to his *Mere Christianity*.

> The contents of this book were first given on the air, and then published in three separate parts as *The Case for Christianity* (1943), *Christian Behaviour* (1943), and *Beyond Personality* (1945). In the printed version I made a few additions to what I had said at the microphone, but otherwise left the text much as it had been. A "talk" on the radio should, I think, be as like real talk as possible, and should not sound like an essay being read aloud. In my talks I had theretofore used all the contractions and colloquialisms I ordinarily use in conversation. In the printed version I reproduced this, putting *don't* and *we've* for *do not* and *we have*. And wherever, in the talks, I had made the importance of a word clear by the emphasis of my voice, I printed it in italics. I am now inclined to think that this was a mistake—an undesirable hybrid between the art of speaking and the art of writing. A talker ought to use variations of voice for emphasis because

his medium naturally lends itself to that method: but a writer ought not to use italics for the same purpose. He has his own, different, means of bringing out the key words and ought to use them. In this edition I have expanded the contractions and replaced most of the italics by recasting the sentences in which they occurred: but without altering, I hope, the "popular" or "familiar" tone which I had all along intended.

Sometimes members of your audience won't seem to get any of what you are saying. Others may receive it correctly at the moment, but the human memory is so poor that only minutes later several components of the message will have simply been lost and no longer available to a listener's consciousness.

I learned very early in my experience as a speaker—as distinguished from an entertainer—that if there were five hundred individuals present, they were perceiving not one Steve Allen at the lectern, but five hundred separate me's.

To give just a few illustrations:

A young woman, to whose father I might bear a physical resemblance, might perceive me primarily as a male, to some degree physically attractive.

An elderly conservative Republican gentleman in the front row might perceive me primarily as a notorious Democrat or liberal.

A tailor in the audience might perceive me as someone attired unfashionably.

A fan of my television comedy program might perceive me as too stuffy and serious on this particular occasion.

A poorly educated person might perceive me as someone who uses too many big words.

One of my sons might perceive me as just "Dad."

My wife might perceive me as having put on a bit too much weight recently.

I expressed this same insight, some years ago, in the following poem:

Lover's Question

I am an infant to my mother
I am a captain to my crew
I am a hero to my children
    What am I to you?

I am a jawbone to my dentist
And a gentile to the Jew
I am a stranger to a stranger
    What am I to you?

    I am no one thing to myself
    Were I alone I'd not exist
    To a giant I'm an elf
    To the mouse a mailed fist.

Though I'm an ancient to a yearling
    To the old I'm someone new
I'm a white man to the Negro
    What am I to you?

    I am no one thing alone,
    To the nervous shrew I'm unction
    To my blood I'm flesh and bone
    I relatively function.

To the beggar I'm a donor
    By the slave considered free
Love, complete the strange mosaic:
    What think you of me?

To return to our point: Since your message is going to have to get through a number of psychological roadblocks, you would be well advised to keep the message itself as clear as possible.

In Summation

One benefit of reading a book of this sort is that you will, in the future, be better protected against the calculated devices, sometimes even deceptions, of other speakers. It would be fortunate if all public address was intended to enlighten, instruct, or inspire. In reality it is often used to sell, to convince others by the virtue of the speaker's argument, or to confuse by a sort of verbal sleight-of-hand. After reading this book you will be better able to distinguish between sound and unsound arguments, to be on guard against such despicable devices as the *ad hominem* attack—in which an individual, rather than his argument, is the target—the mind-reading fallacy, and others. Through consideration of such shoddy methods you will hopefully come to appreciate that in order to speak well it will be necessary for you to learn to write well, or at least better than you do presently. And to write and speak well you must learn something about *thinking*, about logical reasoning. There is, after all, more to effective public speaking than simply gabbling on for the designated period of time.

Chapter 3

Rehearsing the Speech

The rehearsing you will be required to do falls into two categories: rehearsing your speech and rehearsing your mouth. The difference here is partly psychological, since—obviously—it will eventually be your mouth that will give voice to your speech. But before your mouth can do a good job of that it will have to be better than it probably is at present at the basic human act of speaking. The problem, you see, is that on the lecture platform you won't be able to get away with the sort of bad habits that, being human—and being American—you have almost certainly fallen into. It may occur to you that if you intend to do nothing at the lectern but read your speech your slovenly habits, if any, in daily conversation have no relevance. Forget that; they do. The reason is that even if you are a natural-born speech reader, you will inevitably do a certain amount of speaking, once introduced, in addition to whatever you might have planned or put on paper. Circumstances always alter cases, and since you will have to do some ad-libbing you might as well make this portion of your total address conform to the more formal part of it.

That being the case, you might find some use in an exercise I developed when I was twenty-one and first working in radio, in Phoenix, Arizona. There was no problem in reading commercials or other scripted materials, but even then, as a lowly local radio announcer, I had to do a certain amount of ad-libbing, even if it was just identifying the station, giving the correct time, suggesting that listeners stay tuned for the following program, and so on. And there were occasional assignments—sports events, parades, interviews—where scripts were not provided. The solution was to use my car as a rehearsal studio. As I drove about the city I would simply give a "play-by-play" description of whatever I was watching. It sounded something like this:

> Here we are again, folks, as I continue my description of the things and people and places I see as I drive around good old Phoenix, Arizona. It's slightly rainy out this morning, which is pretty unusual for this time of year and—come to thing of it—for this part of the country, which is essentially desert, as you know. But in any event I now see, as I pass the corner of Fourth and Jefferson, two elderly women about to cross the street, waiting for the light to change. One of them is walking a small poodle. At least, I think it's a poodle, although I'm not sure it's pure-blooded. On my right now as I proceed along I see a hardware store, a bakery shop, and a place that sells Indian turquoise jewelry.

As you can see, there was nothing the least bit noteworthy about what I was saying. However, it was providing invaluable practice at communicating the impressions made upon me.

You may choose to emulate my example by using your automobile as a private rehearsal studio, but there is no reason to limit yourself to that physical context. You can perform the same sort of simple exercise almost anywhere you find yourself. The next time you're at home alone, for example, make the "play-by-play" experiment by simply describing to an imaginary audience what you are doing or experiencing at the moment. A sample monologue might go as follows:

Good morning, ladies and gentlemen. I'm broadcasting to you from my house here at 314 West Simpson Street, and my purpose at the moment is just to tell you what is going on here in my kitchen. It's not the most fascinating thing in the world, I guess, but you might find it of moderate interest.

For example, in the background you might be able to detect the sound of our washing machine, inasmuch as my wife put a load in about fifteen minutes ago and I'm just hanging around at the moment waiting to turn the machine off for her, since she had to go visit her mother.

I'm also making my own breakfast just now, which consists of corn flakes with a little skimmed milk, a sliced banana, and honey instead of white sugar. Both my wife and I are, if not actually health food nuts, at least people who eat a sensible and well-balanced diet.

At the moment I'm looking at our kitchen window, because I've noticed that a couple of birds have settled on the sill. I don't know what kind they are—sparrows, perhaps—but every year at this time they seem to be fairly common here in the neighborhood.

That's more than enough to give you the idea. Don't be in the least concerned with making your account dramatic or "interesting." At this stage of your development as a public speaker, the purpose of the exercise is not to thrill or fascinate an audience (there is none) but simply to keep your own mouth working in as intelligible and coherent a manner as possible. Don't be put off by the fact that when you first start this sort of exercise you "feel dumb." Of course you do; there is an inherently absurd element to the business of speaking aloud in an empty room. But that element is not of the slightest importance in the context of your purpose. Needless to say, if during the simple description of what you're seeing in your immediate environment you also happen to have a profound thought or two—include it in your remarks. But nothing of the sort is at all necessary.

Realize that a speech is, among other things, a performance. It is something you do in front of an audience. Not even the world's greatest actor would dream of walking on stage without long periods of rehearsal. So you, too, should allow time for a period of preparation. Common sense will tell you how much should be set aside for the task. Obviously, for a five-minute speech you don't have to rehearse for six months. But you'll eventually be sorry if you don't rehearse at all.

Common sense can also dictate the forms your rehearsal might take. The following are some of the possibilities:

1. Read the speech over several times, silently.

2. Read the speech several times aloud.

3. Practice your delivery, including the entire address, standing in front of a mirror. This gives you the opportunity to observe not only your general attitude but also your gestures, posture, and facial expression.

4. Read the speech into a tape recorder and listen to the results. Then listen to them again. At this stage you will make an astounding discovery. Things begin to become apparent to you at a second listening (or, for that matter, a tenth) that had escaped your attention earlier.

5. If you have access to videotaping equipment, make a record of your performance in that way.

6. If you have cooperative family members, deliver the speech to them and ask for their honest comments. Don't make the mistake of welcoming only compliments and tuning out messages that are analytical or critical. If your spouse says something like "I think it's quite good but you were talking too fast," don't argue the point, whether or not your ego will permit you to agree at that moment. Just absorb the message and let it bounce around in your internal computer.

Beware of the trap of ego-involvement. Once you create something—anything at all: a do-it-yourself chicken coop, a poem, a song, a speech—you make an emotional investment in it. There's no rational reason why you should, and if I were God I wouldn't have created a race that habitually did such stupid things. But as for reality, we are all notorious for our inability to correctly evaluate our own work.

Oddly enough, if you have a weak ego you may occasionally shortchange yourself by being *too* critical of something you've done, but such instances are far outnumbered by those in which you will think that your brainchild is more attractive than it really is.

Fortunately, the golden glow of early confidence about the products or our creative labors soon begins to fade. Not only will you be better able to edit your copy if you put it aside for a few days and then take a fresh look at it, but even the passage of a few hours will produce an increased degree of objectivity. And in the meantime do listen to your family or friends, especially if you've asked for their comments.

Again, since all professional speakers rehearse, you should too. In July of 1979, President Carter, who had become sensitive to criticism about his ineffective speaking style, meticulously prepared for an important television address made at the time. He read the text into a pocket tape recorder, played it back repeatedly, videotaped the speech so as to make a personal analysis of his projection, hand gestures, and general speaking style—and, as a result, delivered one of his most effective addresses.

Carter is not the only recent president to seek professional assistance for his inadequate speaking style. There is a moderately amusing story of another who did so.

Back in 1961, after seven years of doing comedy programs for NBC, I did our show for one season on the ABC television network. In addition to Louis Nye, Don Knotts, Pat Harrington, Tom Poston, and other familiar faces, we introduced that year two newcomers who have since gone on to well-deserved success: Tim Conway and Jim Nabors. The Smothers Brothers were also members of our comedy family on the ABC show.

Another one of our company was a young fellow named Don Penny, a comic who impressed me as a sort of teenage Eddie Cantor, although he was no longer a teenager. He was a bright young fellow although, for whatever reasons, he did not subsequently have the success enjoyed by many other comedians who worked on my TV shows of the 1950s and 1960s. I did not, in fact, hear anything further of Don for quite a few years thereafter. Then, one day during the time when Gerald Ford was settling into the presidency in the aftermath of the Watergate scandal, I came across a syndicated feature article in *The Los Angeles Times*. It explained that the President, perhaps having become sensitive to jokes by Chevy Chase and other comedians about his somewhat bumbling manner at the podium, had not only enlisted a professional to instruct him in how to conduct himself at the lectern, but had, in fact, moved the instructor into the White House and given him his own office. The expert was, of course, our old friend, comedian Don Penny. Although the notion of a former comedian instructing the most powerful man in the world, an American president, in how to conduct himself when addressing the inhabitants of planet Earth is slightly bizarre, it dramatizes the high premium that today's office holders—and seekers—place on effectiveness at public speaking.

My own view concerning President Carter's disastrous drop in the popularity polls, after the honeymoon period of his first year in office, is that it was caused by the lightweight image he projected as a speaker more than by any specific failures of presidential policy. I did, in fact, foresee that inasmuch as Ronald Reagan was almost certain to be the Republican presidential candidate, a dangerous situation was looming for the Democrats. This has absolutely nothing to do with issues or political philosophies. It is simply that because of his professions as radio announcer and actor, Reagan was far more effective on the platform than almost any lifelong professional politician. It is significant that he was not nearly so effective when spontaneously answering questions from the press as when delivering his standard speech. But it did not require much exercise of the imagination to envision a situation in which Reagan, with his rich, practiced actor's voice, would easily overpower Carter, with his soft-spoken, high-pitched, almost mumbling, southern-rural delivery.

Learning from Others

Also starting during your rehearsal phase, check the competition. (If you want to learn to ice skate, it makes sense to watch superior skaters in action. If you're studying the piano, you'll be well advised to listen to the great pianists. Just so, in public speaking it is wise to study those who are most effective at the craft.) Ask yourself exactly what it is about their speechmaking that you approve of. The voice? The manner? The vocabulary? The element of humor? The speaker's facial expressions, gestures, relaxation, forcefulness, passion?

The same drama was repeated in 1984 when Reagan had the good fortune to find himself opposed by Walter Mondale, a man of far greater compassion and many more years of political experience but—alas for the hopes of his party—a lackluster speaker.

Senator Gary Hart would have done better against Reagan, not because he was any more deserving of being elected president, but simply because he is more effective on the lecture platform. The strong impression that New York Governor Mario Cuomo made at the Democratic convention was due in part to the content of his message but to a far greater extent to the ease, naturalness, and warmth of his speaking style.

Oddly enough, you can also learn a great deal from inept speakers. Ask again: Precisely *why* do you rate them as ineffectual? Do they speak in a halting and partially incoherent manner? Do they keep their eyes cast down on a fully written text, rarely making audience contact? Do they mispronounce some words and slur others? Is their tone of voice weak, grating, or otherwise unattractive? Do they seem to have an inadequate grasp of their subject? Do they have distracting nervous mannerisms such as inappropriate gestures, brow mopping, facial tics, or grimaces?

Do they—and there is some awkwardness in bringing up the point—have dialects or accents so pronounced that they might be considered unappealing by members of an audience who come from different social or regional backgrounds? Whether we are charitable and compassionate in making such judgments or not, the fact is that most of us react negatively to certain regional or class dialects.

Many accents of the American South fall very pleasingly indeed on the ear. Men with such speech patterns may seem especially masculine; women, delightfully feminine. But there are other southern accents which are as pleasant to the ear of most disinterested listeners as the sound of fingernails on a blackboard. Indeed, such accents are almost never encountered in the context of the lecture platform, radio, film, television, or the theater unless they are employed for comic effect.

This is not merely a matter of regional bias or social class, because New England accents, too, may be divided into the appealing and the unappealing. The now fortunately somewhat rare "Harvard accent," with its suggestion of clenched jaws and a sort of forced, rigid dignity, has often been spoofed by comedy actors, and with good reason. Even in individual cities there are varieties of dialect. An upper-class Boston accent is pleasant, but lower-class speech patterns heard in the same setting often sound harsh, strident, unmelodious. Other regional and local dialects that are often considered unattractive may be heard in certain parts of Texas and in New York's Bronx and Brooklyn neighborhoods.

Overcoming Dialects, Accents, and Other Impediments

But what if you happen to speak with some such dialect? Is your case hopeless? Not at all. The simple act of traveling a good deal, or living for a time in another part of the country, often works wonders. If that is not possible, a speech therapist can be consulted. Probably the best method of all to at least tone down an accent, if it is of the objectionable sort, is to pay careful attention to those radio and television voices that are obviously in the pleasant-to-hear category: Walter Cronkite, Diane Sawyer, Dan Rather, Morley Safer, Mike Wallace, Edwin Newman, Jane Pauley, Bill Moyers, George Will, or whatever newscasters, actors, or entertainers might be noted for their easy-to-listen-to speaking style. Beware, however, of patterning yourself after the peculiar, unnatural, singsong voices of some women who read the news on radio and television. Comedienne Jane Curtin, of the original *Saturday Night Live* family, did a marvelous imitation of such voices when she used to do the newscast sketches with Dan Aykroyd or Chevy Chase.

But what if you have an actual speech impediment or a physical problem that makes your voice sound odd? Does this mean you must forego the speechmaker's art? No, it does not. I once interviewed a gentleman on television who had achieved remarkable success in the business world, even though he suffered from the condition known as harelip. TV interviewer Barbara Walters speaks with a slight lisp. Talk-show host Jack Paar had a severe stuttering problem as a young man. Author Truman Capote had an unfortunate voice intonation but was an interesting speaker nevertheless.

If your own speech impediment is severe enough, you might want to make some casual, even humorous reference to it at the outset of your remarks, by way of relieving the tension of your listeners. The same point might be considered if you suffer from some physical incapacity that does not specifically affect your speech. If, for example, you have unusually poor vision, are a paraplegic, have to walk with crutches, or something of this sort, such a factor can actually concentrate the attention of an audience. Again, it can be helpful to make some quick passing reference to your predicament. A severely crippled speaker, for example, might—after struggling to the platform—say, "As you can see, it took me considerably longer to get here than it did the first two speakers. To tell you the truth, it's not all that much fun walking up those steps and making my way across the stage. Nevertheless, I wanted very much to do that because I have something quite important to say."

To sum up, there are ways that even negative factors can be employed to productive effect.

Memorizing a Speech

You memorize by repeated rehearsal: practice, practice, practice. Some experts on the art of public speaking, however, are horrified by the very prospect of memorizing a speech. Art Linkletter, for example, states his feelings plainly enough: "You should never, never, try to memorize an entire speech word-for-word."

For most speakers Art's advice will be perfectly sound. However, as is the case with all rules, there are exceptions to Art's rule, too. There *is* the one obvious danger of the memorization process that if you suddenly forget a line you can be in deep trouble. But even then you need not panic if you're familiar with the subject matter. A simple solution is to memorize your speech, if you prefer, but also go on stage fortified by some sort of paper backup. It may be either a copy of the speech, which you need not look at, or some Ronald Reagan-type outline on 3 x 5 or 5 x 7 cards.

Memorizing short speeches is obviously much easier than memorizing long ones. Memorizing anything longer than ten pages, in fact, is difficult and time-consuming, even for professional actors. The point here is not to recommend the process, but merely to let you know it is one more option available to you.

Even if you have memorized a speech there's no reason you have to stick to it once the ballgame actually starts. When you're in the middle of page seven, for example, a perfectly fascinating digression or addendum to your case may occur to you. No problem; simply express yourself on the point and then return to your text.

An excellent aid to memorization is the audiotape recorder. In the old days, reel-to-reel tapes were used for this purpose, but the modern cassettes, including the minicassette, are superior because they can be played in small, pocket-sized recorders and, consequently, carried with you in cars, buses, airplanes, and other places where you would be unlikely to use bulky recording equipment.

Another good thing about memorizing material with the aid of recording is that you can listen while you are engaged in other tasks—swimming (the recorder sits on the poolside deck), lying in bed, shaving or brushing your teeth, having breakfast, jogging, or just relaxing. Don't assume, of course, that just two or three plays of the tape will impress the material on your consciousness. Nor should you think that simply by listening to the tape—even a hundred times—the memorization will be complete. You'll still have to practice aloud, to find out how much you have memorized. But many actors, lecturers, and executives now use such equipment and find it quite helpful. And, as I shall explain later in fuller detail, having the opportunity to hear yourself on tape will enable you to judge your performance in a way that would be impossible otherwise.

You'll never guess what I'm going to tell you to do if you choose to memorize your speech completely: *Don't* deliver it exactly as memorized. The remembered form will be in your mind, obviously enough. It's just that it should not become a rigid prison restricting your imagination but should, rather, serve as a strong basis from which you may creatively depart.

If, for reasons of time limitation, you haven't been able to memorize your entire address, then give particular attention to the opening and closing. If you make it clear to your audience at the outset that you are communicating with them directly, in a personal way, they will, perhaps, not notice when you later begin to read from the text. If you finish in the same manner, with no downward glances, that will leave the same impression.

Should You Just Read Your Speech?

Some speakers are most effective when reading a prepared text. Others excel at entirely extemporaneous speech, and still others at speaking from an outline or a series of notes. Since most of those who are required to address audiences with reasonable frequency must at times speak formally and at other times informally, you should analyze your abilities, not as a public speaker per se—since that is quite a broad term—but in the various categories just mentioned.

First, then, consider speaking from a prepared text.

If you are an important business executive, a civic official, or a leader of any other kind, you may be fortunate enough to have others available to prepare your formal remarks. This must often be done, for example, for politicians, who are simply too busy to write all their own speeches. There is nothing peculiarly American about this. It has been necessary throughout history in the cases of prime ministers, kings, popes, and other dignitaries. Most speakers, of course, will not be so fortunate as to have ghost-writers. But whoever writes it, *you're* going to have to rehearse and deliver it.

There are obvious advantages to reading a speech. You don't have to worry about the danger of forgetting anything, you'll know how long your speech will take, your argument will be better developed than if you were just ad-libbing, and so on. But there is also a danger. Like almost all negatives, it can be overcome but it must be faced. I refer to the fact that most people—including some experienced lecturers—have great difficulty in *sounding natural* when they are reading. God knows why; there is certainly no logical reason. But even some professional actors have trouble speaking in a natural manner when the very same sorts of things they have been saying all their lives get put down on paper. They have little difficulty in declaiming Shakespeare, acting out highly emotional scenes in which they may be called upon to shout, weep, exhibit anger, fear, or other forms of passion. But they seem unable to sound like actual human beings if they are called upon to *read* such simple lines as "Hello, Charlie" or "I wonder what time it is" or "Could you please pass the salt?"

It's important, as I say, for you to grasp this fact if you have already decided that, for your first few speeches at least, you'll be working from a script. That's perfectly all right. It does give you a certain measure of security as you launch your public speaking career. But unless you're one of those rare individuals whose natural style on the platform is that of everyday discourse, you'll simply have to do a good deal of rehearsing, ideally with a tape recorder, to make your delivery as natural as possible. Nothing makes an audience restless faster than a dull, dry, artificial, monotonous voice, no matter how fascinating the words appear to be on paper.

One odd thing that happens to speakers who have difficulty reading in a natural way is that they may pronounce the word *a* (which is properly pronounced *uh*) as if it were spelled *ay*, and the word *the* (properly pronounced *thuh*) as if it were spelled *thee*.

One of the factors of naturalness, of course, is pace, the speed at which you speak. If you speak too slowly—or too quickly—you will sound unnatural. So check this point carefully when you listen to tape recordings of your rehearsals. Are you speaking at the same approximate rate of words per minute that you employ in normal conversation? If not, make the necessary change accordingly.

Needless to say, the effect of naturalness is achieved not only in the act of speaking but even earlier, in the act of writing. So in forming your sentences, paragraphs, and pages beware of grandiose or artificial phrases unless you happen to be to the manner born and that is your natural conversational style.

I have one final recommendation for rehearsing. If your town has one of those record shops that feature a poetry, drama, or lecture department, you might be able to locate recordings by gifted speakers. Some libraries, too, have recorded material of this sort. If you live in a smaller community, or your budget won't permit such expenditures, seek out speakers who appear on radio or television. Listening to such material can be quite helpful during your own rehearsal stage.

Chapter 4

Getting
Ready

A great deal of the important work of speechmaking takes place before you ever go near the platform, just as the bulk of the work that athletes do does not occur during the actual games but during the long years of preparation. The more work you do in advance, the more relaxed, confident, and able you'll be at the lectern.

Do your homework.

You might, for example, learn something about public speaking by visiting one of those nightclubs—now common around the country—that present chiefly new young comedians. You may see eight or ten or a dozen of them perform in an evening, with each allotted about ten minutes. Even though they are dealing in humor and not making formal speeches, you can learn a number of things from them. First, you will notice that almost all of them speak in a relaxed, conversational manner, rather than with the old-fashioned, rapid-fire, show-biz delivery of the comedians of the nineteen thirties, forties, and fifties. This is an important lesson. Learn it well.

You are fortunate, in one respect, that you are doing your public speaking at this particular point in history, for—again—the most effective speakers of the present day are those who employ a chiefly natural, conversational tone. The old-style William Jennings Bryan or Bible-thumping form of address is pretty much out, except in rare circumstances.

How to Spend—and Not Spend— the Hours Before Your Speech

The rules on this point are nothing more than common sense. Although speechmaking is not one of life's most strenuous activities, it does make demands on your nervous system. Accordingly, it makes no sense to arrive at the big moment in a state of physical exhaustion from having stayed up partying all night, having had too much wine, beer, or liquor, or—if you're made nervous by caffeine—drinking excessive amounts of coffee, tea, or cola beverages. Make arrangements to get the proper amount of sleep before the event and, if possible, set aside time for at least a few minutes' rest, at your hotel or home, before your talk. As for cocktail parties, try to avoid them. But if there is no way that can be done, then ask that they be scheduled after, rather than before, your address. If the audience spends time with you before your talk, that may take the edge off such excitement as your physical presence may create. Also, carrying on conversations, however brief, with dozens of people can sap energy that you ought to be conserving for the important task ahead.

One of the several blessings of serving as speaker is that you are usually not expected to take part in the deadly ritual known as the cocktail hour. I greatly enjoy the company of my fellow humans, and consider few experiences as pleasurable as spending an evening in the stimulating company of a *small* group of either friends or interesting strangers. But when the guest list numbers more than fifty (and at some gatherings there are hundreds taking part in cocktail receptions), I lose interest. This is because (*a*) it's difficult to hear what any one person is saying when scores are gabbling at the same time, *(b)* it's almost impossible to carry on a coherent conversation when one is subject to constant interruptions, introductions, and changes of subject, and *(c)* I hate cigarette smoke.

If you are just a guest you are probably stuck with this sort of thing, unless you plan to arrive shortly before the dinner hour. But as speaker or master of ceremonies you are perfectly within your rights to explain to the host group that you prefer *not* to take part in the cocktail hour. At certain large formal events, in fact, it is considered so necessary to protect visiting dignitaries from such indignities that they are herded off to a separate room where a small number of them may enjoy each other's company in quiet and privacy.

If you eventually become a speaker considerably in demand, however, you'll discover that some groups can be quite insistent about spending time with you socially. The worst experience of this sort I ever had happened some years ago during an otherwise delightful week spent at the St. Paul Winter Carnival. I was doing a nightly syndicated comedy-and-talk television series at the time, and we originated the show from the Minneapolis-St. Paul area for five days. Before we arrived, one local hostess was kind enough to extend an invitation to a midday cocktail party. After checking our production schedule for that day and finding it hopelessly busy, I instructed a member of my staff to thank the woman profusely but to explain, in detail, why it was impossible for me to have the pleasure of joining her and her guests.

A few days later, while we were still in Los Angeles, somewhat more pressure was applied. The woman, apparently of some standing in Twin Cities society, sent back a message that made her invitation seem almost like a command performance.

Again I told one of our production people to outline—this time by letter—the reasons it was not possible for me to attend the party. One was that we were scheduled to pretape a segment of our show from a small lake nearby. The plan was for me to don a wet suit and breathing apparatus and plunge through a hole in the ice into the water below. When the day came I had quite forgotten about the invitation. I changed out of my own clothing and into a wet suit at some sort of Elks or American Legion lodge close to the lake.

The vice-president in charge of acquiring wet suits had unfortunately neglected to get the proper size. I'm six feet, three inches tall and weigh two hundred pounds. The suit in question was so much too short that I literally had to walk in a stooped-over manner, since it was impossible to straighten up while wearing it. But under the heading of "the show must go on," I submitted to this combination of discomfort and pain, did a brief monologue at the edge of the ice, jumped into the water, got a few laughs, and finished taping the routine.

Since I naturally didn't want my only pair of glasses to accidentally get knocked off and fall to the bottom of the frozen lake, I was not wearing them when I clambered out of the water and flopped down on the ice. At this point two men helped me to my feet and directed me to a small van. In a few seconds I was inside the van—unfortunately, without glasses—and bumping along an ice-rutted road to what I assumed was the lodge where I was supposed to get out of the too-tight wet suit and back into my own clothes. To my surprise the van did not stop at the lodge but made a right turn and bounced off through a nearby stand of trees. Without my glasses I wasn't sure where we were going and for a few minutes didn't give the matter much thought, assuming that someone had taken my clothes to a more comfortable spot so that I could make the change there.

A moment later the van stopped. As I climbed out the side door I said to one of the two men, "Where are we?"

"Oh," he said, "this is Mrs. _____'s house. You're going to her party."

"The hell I am," I replied.

The faces of several guests floated past as I walked into the house and was shown up a staircase to a second-story bedroom and bathroom. Neither of the men, it developed, had brought my glasses. I struggled uncomfortably out of the wet suit and in a few minutes stood in the locked bathroom—naked, without glasses, without clothing to put on, and of course without the slightest possibility of going downstairs, even if I had wanted to.

For quite a long time I heard no signs of life except the distant chatter of cocktail-party conversation on the lower floor. Eventually an unidentified male voice called through the door, "How are you doing in there?"

"I'm sitting here naked," I answered, "because I have no clothes to put on. Nor do I have my eyeglasses."

"Oh," was the response.

Another twenty minutes passed, after which one of the men from our show—God knows how he found out where I was—came upstairs carrying my clothes.

"How the hell did you get here?" he asked. "We've been looking for you."

"I got here," I explained, "because the idiot woman refused to take no for an answer and had me literally kidnapped and brought here. Unfortunately for her purposes, nobody brought my clothing, so I've been unable to mingle with her guests."

I then put on my clothes, was shortly thereafter reunited with my eyeglasses, walked downstairs—without a word to the bystanders, all of whom looked guilty and embarrassed—got into another car, and was driven back to continue working on the television show.

It's unlikely you'll ever suffer such an inconvenience, but practically all professional lecturers have bizarre stories of this general sort to tell.

Your Physical Condition

Simple intelligence will tell you what sorts of things you ought not to eat, or drink, before you take to the platform. Radishes, onions, soda pop, and beer are not indicated. Some vocalists and speakers will not drink milk before a performance because it affects the throat passages.

As regards alcoholic beverages you'll have to make up your own mind. I wouldn't dream of taking a drink before I entertain or lecture, although there are some people who prefer to have a little beer, wine, or perhaps something stronger before they go to the platform. However, a good rule would be "If in doubt, don't do it." The danger of having several drinks before you go on stage is that you can end up being a true horse's ass and simply never know it. I once saw this happen to a speaker at a dinner held by the Conference of Christian Athletes. A famous football player of earlier days had simply had too much wine before he got up to the platform. He has since passed away and I'm sure went to his grave never knowing what a dreadful impression he had made. It's funny when Foster Brookes does it, but Foster himself, parenthetically, is not only a nondrinker but an antidrinker. The blurred speech and dopey eyes of the true drunk are pathetic, not amusing, on stage.

Your Attire

It's a minor point not worth extended comment, but you should give thought to the suitability of your attire when speaking in public. The controlling factor should be the general expectations of your audience. In other words, you don't show up at a Holy Name Society Communion Breakfast dressed like Sammy Davis, Jr., or at a bankers' convention wearing blue jeans and a military fatigue jacket, or, if you're a woman, dress the way you might for a glamorous evening on the town. The point is that your clothing should in no way distract.

Familiarizing Yourself with the Setting for Your Speech

Although it is not always possible to do so, there are advantages to familiarizing yourself with the terrain on which you'll be working. If the circumstances permit, walk around the room—not only on the stage but through the audience seating. Sit down in two or three parts of the auditorium so you will know what the speaker's area looks like from out front. If any questions occur to you, *ask* them. You can get valuable information not only from your official hosts but also from busboys, security personnel, electricians, or lighting technicians. You might be able to use such information as the specifics of the menu, whether the room has a spotlight, how well the public address system works, where the nearest restrooms are, and so on.

Lighting

Check out the podium or lectern area to see if there is sufficient light to permit you to read your typewritten pages or notes. Most podiums have a small light just under the top front edge for the speaker's convenience, but about one time in ten the bulb is burned out or the unit isn't plugged in. It's much better to discover such a problem before the ballgame starts. Because my eyes pick up somewhat less light than those of the average person, I generally carry a small pocket flashlight. Every so often it comes in handy for reading papers and notes while lecturing or entertaining.

The speaker should also be lighted, of course. When this detail has not been properly attended to and the speeches have to take place anyway, I always comment on it. On one occasion when I was illuminated by a single harsh overhead bulb, I said,"The last time I saw lighting this bad was at the Nuremberg trials."

On another occasion I said, "This would be great lighting for the reading of a will."

You might also try "I know the hotel is trying to save energy, but this is ridiculous."

Seating

Unless you are made uncomfortable by having an audience quite close to you, you should know that this is the best possible situation for a speaker. It's good for entertainers and for actors in plays, too. All of us prefer to work intimate rooms in which members of the audience are seated quite close to the stage.

Audience contact is more difficult if there is considerable space between you and the first row. All speakers and entertainers hate to work in hotel ballrooms, where—because dancing is planned for later in the evening—there's a vast expanse of empty space in front of the stage, with tables set well back on both sides and in the rear. You might think that if a person were a particularly effective speaker such factors wouldn't matter in the least. But you'd be wrong. They matter. Therefore, if there's any way that your own wishes can control the situation, you should let your hosts know that you would like the first row of tables—or seats, if there's no dining—moved as close to your platform as possible.

Sound

Because of the modern world's general dependence on sound amplification systems, I have often wondered how many people actually heard the important speeches of history, such as the Sermon on the Mount or the Gettysburg Address, particularly when a good many of them are said to have been delivered in an outdoor setting. It is hard enough to hear an unamplified speaker in an enclosed space. The difficulty increases in open air.

Determine, therefore, long before the date of your talk, whether public address equipment is available. If it is you're fortunate, although there are certain problems that present themselves when you're using a microphone. Your mouth should not be too close to the mike, for example. If it is, words with the letter *p* will produce a "popping" sound. But don't speak too far from the microphone, either, or you won't be heard. If in doubt, ask, "Can you hear me all right?" They'll tell you, and may do so even if you don't ask, if your volume is too low.

If there is no PA system it's up to you to make yourself audible to everyone present. There's no problem at all if you're addressing a small audience of seventy five; but if you're in an auditorium that seats two hundred or more, you simply will not be heard beyond the first few rows if you speak in your normal conversational tone of voice.

I have a theory that the art of oratory developed partly because of this acoustical factor. In the long ages before microphones were invented, if a clergyman, civic leader, or military commander was addressing thousands of people, he would have had to sustain his voice level at the shouting range, perhaps for a long period of time. Since shouting is, in almost all other contexts, associated with exaggerated emotion, this could account for the fervor and semi-hysterical tone that has characterized oratory through the centuries.

Don't make the mistake of speaking in an oratorical manner

when a perfectly workable sound system is carrying your voice. However, if you do *not* greatly increase your volume in the absence of such equipment, a portion of your audience will become restless and inattentive. Eventually you'll hear those disconcerting cries of "Louder!" If you're a somewhat hyper, extroverted person you'll have no difficulty adding volume to your spoken message, but most of us tend more toward shyness and introversion as speakers, a fact I know from personal experience.

If you're in doubt as to whether you can be heard in larger rooms, set up an experimental session or two. Take a friend or family member into a large space, take up positions at opposite ends, and begin speaking. The test will be far from scientific; the later addition of three or four hundred clothed bodies will absorb a great many sound waves that, in an empty room, will reach from the front to the back, but at least such an experiment will give you a bit of practice in addressing the problem.

Resolving the Details of Your Presentation

There are, you will be pleased to learn, very few, if any, formal rules for public speaking. Oh, I suppose one could, if one wished, make out an endless list of such rules: Do not fall off the stage. Do not throw up while on the platform. Do not tell dirty jokes at a convent. And so forth. But it really all comes down to common sense.

There are, however, certain decisions about your presentation that you will want to make beforehand. In many cases you may be guided simply by your own preference as to what seems most reasonable in a given situation.

Using a Lectern

The lectern will give you something to "hide behind," or lean on. It definitely provides a measure of psychological assurance. You should therefore ask if one is available. If (as does occur in come rare cases) you're out of luck, I've found that a tall music stand—

the black metal kind—can serve almost as well. You're unlikely to find a music stand in the average restaurant, but high schools, colleges, churches, and theaters often have them.

Where to Look

Some speakers and entertainers find that it helps them to make audience contact if they stare intently into the faces of various individuals seated in the first few rows. Others find that doing so distracts them, if it does not totally petrify them. For my own part I generally do not look at those in the front rows, unless I spy a few faces with that wonderfully rapt, attentive expression from which a speaker can derive supportive feedback. I generally prefer to look at a series of points about three-quarters of the way back into the house.

Your glance should not favor any particular part of the audience or side of the auditorium; those listening to you should have the impression that you are interested in communicating with all of them. This can be achieved simply by directing your glance to various parts of the theater, including the balcony, if there is one.

Practice the art of reading so that you can spend as much time as possible looking out at the audience and as little time as possible with head down and eyes on the printed page. No matter how attractively your hair is styled, no audience in the world will maintain an interest in it for very long. What they want to see is your face, and particularly your eyes.

On those occasions when, for whatever reasons, I must read a speech, I find it helpful to keep a finger on the line I am speaking at any given moment. Then, after I spend a few seconds looking out at the audience, I have no trouble relocating the proper place on the page.

It's easier to read if you underline certain especially significant portions of the speech, using a thick-line felt-tip black pen for the purpose. This is a more important detail than it might at first seem, because the decision as to which words in a given sentence you will vocally emphasize is itself extremely important. The two sentences "*John* hit him" and "John hit *him*" are by no means the same. They have different meanings. Underlining key words, therefore, reminds you of the proper emphasis and helps to add a bit of vocal color to your talk.

You might also draw straight black lines across the page to separate paragraphs, simply to aid the eye.

What About Your Hands?

Some professional actors and entertainers never do become totally at ease with those starfishlike appendages hanging from the ends of their arms. Others never have to face the problem at all. Oddly enough, you've probably given no thought to what to do with your hands since you first discovered them in front of your face in the cradle. The lecturer at least has an easier time of it than the actor, in that the lecturer is usually protected by some sort of lectern, podium, high music stand, or microphone, which he or she may elect to touch or lean against. If you are standing on a stage without such defenses, simply do with your hands what you would if talking to a member of your family. Put one hand in your jacket pocket and gesture with the other. Or—if the occasion is very informal— put them both in your pockets. Scratch your nose if it itches, make a gesture if it illustrates a story or point, or clasp both hands behind your back. It's not a big deal unless you make it one.

It's possible, of course, that you are in that small category of public speakers who just can't seem to get their hands and mouths coordinated. Oddly enough, even some successful political figures have this problem. Richard Nixon's gestures always looked a bit puppetlike, and sometimes we see announcers or others on television whose hand movements are so inappropriate that they distract from, rather than enhance, the spoken message. If you are in this category it's far better not to make any gestures at all.

Just as your tone and volume of voice must be related to the size of the auditorium in which you are performing, so must your gestures. A vigorous waving of arms and shaking of fists that might be perfectly suited to a speech delivered at the Los Angeles Coliseum or Madison Square Garden would obviously be totally out of place at a luncheon meeting in a small motel coffee shop.

Props, Notes, and Supportive Literature

If you're one of those rare individuals who, despite the best advice, is still faced with the what-to-do-with-my-hands problem, you might resort to the use of props. This is a trick that professional actors and actresses learn early in the game. The next time you see a play, film, or television drama, note the objects the performers touch or handle. They may employ guns, tennis rackets, pocket combs, books, eyeglasses, cigars, crocheting paraphernalia, a beer glass, a football, a coffee cup—any of the thousands of objects with which people normally come into contact.

I'm naturally not suggesting that you stand on the speaker's platform with a pistol or tennis racket in your hand. But there are items you can naturally employ in the context of your assignment: typed pages, index cards, a pointer, a pen, an object you might be talking about. Some talk-show hosts hold 5 x 7 cards in their hands while conducting interviews. William F. Buckley holds a clipboard, with notes attached.

It will be better if you don't have to depend on such props, but—if you feel the need, feel free.

In some instances, depending on the complexity and seriousness of your subject, you may wish to bring additional notes, pamphlets, or clippings from which to quote, or to hold aloft as evidence supporting your argument. Some years ago I was invited by the women connected with a prominent temple in Los Angeles to debate Dr. Edward Teller (who has been called "The Father of the H-Bomb") on the subject of American nuclear weapons policy. We sat side by side on the platform. I would naturally not have presumed to debate Teller about matters technical or scientific, but as regards questions of foreign policy and the immorality of large-scale incineration of innocent civilians I was, of course, as qualified as the distinguished physicist.

Just before he was introduced, Dr. Teller glanced down and saw on my lap a small book by Albert Schweitzer, another by Bertrand Russell, and a few religious pamphlets.

"I see you came very well prepared," he whispered, with a slight smile.

"Listen," I said, "if I were really well prepared would I need all this stuff?"

Turning the Pages

Because typists sometimes gather pages together with either a staple or a paper clip, it is possible that you might sometime arrive at the lectern with the pages of your talk fastened together. That's a no-no. Your audience will become aware or distracted if you start fingering paper clips or ripping pages off the staple one by one.

There is no right or wrong system for turning pages. Do whatever is easy for you personally. Some speakers, as they finish each page, move it to the bottom of the pile. Others prefer to turn the pages over in book fashion, placing finished pages upside down to the left of the manuscript. It doesn't matter to me if you crumple up each sheet and stuff it in your mouth, although I suppose this could be inconvenient if you're going to give the same talk again in the future. The important point is to plan this detail in advance. The less ad-libbing you have to do on the platform, particularly during your first few speeches, the better.

If, despite all your fears and careful preparations, something does indeed go wrong at the presentation of your speech, you still don't have to worry about it. First of all, it's highly unlikely that the incident will be in fact as serious as it seems to you. In my own experience I learned years ago that a disaster (one of moderate proportions, at least) could be an enormous help to me. My case is perhaps unique in that I use such mistakes and accidents to get laughs. Even a serious speaker, however, can do the same. If, let's say, you happen to trip walking across the stage or coming up the steps to the platform, you might quip, "I had an interesting trip coming here tonight, but not as interesting as the one I had just now."

If your notes blow off the lectern, the microphone falls off the stage, or something of the sort, you might say, "A few years ago there was reference to one prominent public speaker who—it was said—couldn't chew gum and talk at the same time. Well, I've just discovered I can't give a speech and handle my notes at the same time."

In such circumstances you don't have to be as witty as Voltaire or Mark Twain to get a sympathetic response from your audience.

Chapter 5

The Actual Performance

Your Presentation

Beginning the Speech

If you're to any degree ill at ease—which you probably will be—you may feel under obligation to start speaking the moment you reach the lectern or microphone. But there is no such requirement. There's nothing at all wrong with giving the audience a moment or two to look you over. You may wish to adjust the microphone, place your papers on the speaker's stand, look about the room, perhaps smile slightly, take a relaxing breath or two, put on or take off your glasses.

Again, if we make the assumption that you have had no particular difficulty communicating with others—family, loved ones, friends, acquaintances, strangers—for the past twenty, thirty, or forty years, then it follows that you are already an experienced speaker. Simply address your audience as if it consisted not of hundreds of individuals but of one person who had come prepared to learn something from you.

Suppose, for example, that you're an expert on the game of tennis. A friend says, "Say, you know a lot about tennis and I don't know the first thing about it. Could you just take about ten minutes, starting from scratch, and explain the game to me?" You would simply start right in and never give the slightest thought as to how effective a speaker you were going to be. You would not, in that sort of context, think of yourself at all. You would simply think of (a) the game of tennis and (b) teaching your friend about it. That's the approach to take in addressing an audience.

Naturally not every one of your speaking engagements will cast you in the role of expert and the audience as a collection of ignoramuses, but your speaking style can be the same in either case.

So, all right, let's say you're off and running, your text neatly typed, before you on the lectern. Perhaps you plan to open with a joke. Well, the one portion of your speech that you absolutely must not read is the joke or funny story, if you have chosen to use one. Before your appearance read it over several times, rehearse it aloud, and commit it approximately to memory. An approximate memorization is, believe it or not, better than a literal one, because when you tell the story it should flow with the same ease that would characterize your delivery if you were sharing the anecdote with a friend on a park bench or at a backyard barbecue.

Suiting Your Manner of Speaking to the Content of Your Message

With some TV and radio newsreaders it doesn't seem to matter what sort of story they are relating. Whether it's an amusing item, news about an athletic event, or a report of a tragic fire at an orphanage, they deliver the message in the same mechanical way. Some lecturers make the same mistake. The solution is not for you to try to become as effective at emoting as Al Pacino or Jane Fonda. You don't have to act. But common sense tells you that if you're relating an amusing story you do so in an appropriate tone of voice— and if, on the other hand, you're discussing some sobering or tragic social reality, your manner of speech and the expression on your face must somehow harmonize with what you are saying.

Oratory, as such, is almost a lost art, partly because, in the modern world, it's a generally inappropriate form of personal communication. There are exceptions, of course. Political conventions and campaigns provide certain, if limited, opportunities for florid, passionate speechmaking. So do campaigns for social reform. When people wish to say, "Up with this!" or "Down with that!" they often want to hear strong messages of leadership and inspiration.

But in a far larger percentage of cases, a more low-key, conversational manner is preferable. One of the masters of this sort of speaking was the late Bishop Fulton J. Sheen. Like Arthur Godfrey, Dave Garroway, and other effective communicators of early television in the 1950s, Sheen gave the at-home viewer the impression that he was speaking to him or her alone. His piercing eyes and polished speaking style helped, of course. But the most important factor was the intimate, natural way he spoke.

Billy Graham is also a gifted speaker, but to be most effective he needs a large in-person audience. Like most Protestant clergymen he speaks in a rather old-fashioned, emotional style, but nevertheless commands the listener's attention and drives home his messages forcefully. The Reverend Bob Schuller, Oral Roberts, Reverend Ike, and other TV stars of the religious circuit are also effective communicators.

It might be assumed from such examples that all clergymen are gifted speakers, but this is not at all the case. A good many, particularly those from southern rural backgrounds, speak in a style they must have heard in their own childhoods: the florid, Bible-thumping, southern-fundamentalist-preacher type of oratory which, though it can rouse some audiences to frenzy, is nevertheless remarkably unlike normal American speech. Such orators often have peculiar mannerisms. They may pronounce the word *Jesus* as *Jesus-uh*, or *God* as *God-uh*. They tend to shout and to sound rather hysterical. Often what they're actually communicating is an air of certainty rather than factual information, and this in an area where true certainty is notoriously difficult to achieve. Such speakers appeal chiefly to the kind of people Eric Hoffer described as True Believers.

In the Germany of the 1930s, Adolph Hitler was just such a

speaker. He shouted, raged, stamped his feet, waved his arms, and appealed to the emotions, not the rational faculties, of the German people. One of these emotions was, of course, patriotism.

From this unhappy example you can, nevertheless, learn something about effective public speaking. While it would no doubt be better for the world if you could always truly instruct and enlighten your audiences, the fact is that you will often get more applause and cheers by appealing to their passions and prejudices—sometimes, sadly, even their hatreds. That is why speeches of the older sort abound with such phrases as "the American people," "our great country," "all across this mighty nation," "our brave fighting men," "the insidious enemies of our American way of life," and so on. Patriotism is indeed sometimes a refuge for scoundrels, and by no means only the last.

Getting Emotionally Involved

Although the day of blatant and usually artificial appeals to emotion from the speaker's platform are happily mostly past, this does not mean that the other extreme will always be appropriate. If your subject matter is one that has emotional components, it is perfectly reasonable to make such factors part of your presentation.

Joseph R. Brown, former executive director of the Indian Association for Mental Health, sometimes relates two moving stories which make an important point about the mental health movement in a more effective way than statistics or exhortations might. The first is as follows:

> One of the adopters of a "forgotten" patient had written to ask if she could have a different patient to write to because her patient had never answered. One of the nurses responded to the point of this letter. The nurse said that this patient reacted strongly to the letters from this volunteer whom she had never seen and would probably never see. When a letter arrived, she came out of her deep depression and for two or three days she would communicate freely about the letters she had received and about what was going on around her, but then gradually she would slip back.

These letters coming every couple of weeks had been of substantial help to this nurse in her effort to work with the patient. She pleaded that the volunteer continue . . .

In another case in Indianapolis:

. . . A volunteer was able to visit her adopted patient from time to time. She would stop in for five to ten minutes every week. In the course of two years of visiting, the patient *never* spoke to her. She might indicate she needed a pair of socks, or something of the sort, but she never said a word directly to our adopter.

One afternoon when the volunteer adopter arrived the patient was not in the ward as usual, and the attendant said that she had been taken to the "sick hospital." The adopter thought about driving on home immediately to meet her children and get supper, but as it happens in this particular state hospital the road back to town goes right by the "sick hospital," and so she stopped in. As she approached the bed her footsteps, perhaps familiar to this patient, induced the patient to pull the sheet down from over her face where it had been for some time. She looked up at the adopter as she walked up to the bed. Then she reached out and grabbed the adopter's hand and held it to her cheek and said, "*I knew you would come.*"

I would like to ask you a simple question. Do you think anyone could have ever persuaded this individual volunteer to work as hard for better legislation and for decent appropriations as she is now willing to work? This woman said, "If I work at this program for the rest of my life, I was more than repaid that afternoon. I'll be glad to do everything I can, in any way I can . . ."

We all know people who are, by nature, more emotional than the norm. When they are angry there is no doubt about it. When they are enjoying themselves they make that very clear, too. Others may be more reticent, if not downright shy.

Ordinarily your audience will respond more favorably to your message if they sense that you, personally, have an emotional investment in it. One has to exercise good judgment about this, however. Modern audiences generally react negatively to speakers who seem semihysterical or more excited about the issue than seems reasonable.

Cheerful, upbeat emotion is, of course, more acceptable than negative, critical, or angry emotion. If you want to inspire an audience to help with a fund-raising drive or take part in some other worthy social campaign, the emotional vibrations you transmit should be such as to express your own cheerfulness, enthusiasm, and optimism about the outcome.

There are, of course, certain rare situations—for example, those connected with war or revolution—when the bloody flag must be waved and the mob incited to attack the enemy ramparts. But you're unlikely ever to have such an experience, so the possibility need not be dwelt upon here.

Whatever your honest emotions on the lecture platform are, it is perfectly all right to reveal them. The audience will identify with you, sympathize, and—in most cases—like you better for it. There are even rare situations where it's perfectly all right to confess that you are nervous or to use some equivalent of the old line "Unaccustomed as I am to public speaking . . ."

Perhaps you are following another speaker who has just displayed the combined eloquence of Julius Caesar, Patrick Henry, and Jack Kennedy. The audience—I assure you—will feel for you in that kind of situation. You might try an old line of Milton Berle's: "I wouldn't give a spot like this to a leopard."

But emotional factors should be introduced only if they are relevant. If they are, they can add power to your message.

My wife, Jayne Meadows, is an eloquent speaker, partly because she does invest a great deal of emotion in the task. Some years ago, when she traveled about the country giving talks on behalf of the National Institute for Mental Health, she showed she had the ability to bring audiences to tears, and in every case to inspire and arouse them. This was partly because she cared so much about the subject herself and partly because she would sometimes be moved to tears in relating one particularly tragic story or another. Audiences invariably respond warmly to the emotion she conveys.

The appeal to emotion is particularly effective when the speaker seeks nothing for himself but asks us to care about others. A superb example of such moral exhortation was given by Jean de Sismondi, a Swiss historian and economist. His justly praised argument on behalf of the poverty-stricken factory workers of the nineteenth century, though it was composed in the form of an essay, serves as a perfect example of the highest purpose to which the rhetorical arts may be put: to stimulate moral concern in the public mind. In considering the following brief quotation from that essay, the reader should be aware of the outrageous conditions in which the poor in the England and France of the Industrial Revolution suffered. Not only did they have to labor incredibly long hours for meager wages but they enjoyed practically none of the benefits that American and other workers around the world now take for granted.

Parenthetically it may be noted that such benefits have never been granted out of nothing more than the prodding of a generous nature on the part of the socially powerful. But in any event here is a virtuous member of the upper class speaking with admirable compassion and eloquence.

On whatever side we look, the same lesson meets us everywhere: protect the poor; and it ought to be the most important study of the legislator and of the government.

Protect the poor, for, in consequence of their precarious condition, they cannot contend with the rich without losing every day some of their advantages.

Protect the poor, that they may keep by law, by custom, by a perpetual contract, rather than by competition—the source of rivalry and hatred—that share of the income of the community which their labour ought to secure to them.

Protect the poor, for they want support, that they may have some leisure, some intellectual development, in order to advance in virtue.

Protect the poor, for the greatest danger to law, public

peace and stability is the belief of the poor that they are oppressed, and their hatred of government.

Protect the poor, if you wish industry to flourish, for the poor are the most important consumers.

Protect the poor, if your revenue requires to be increased, for after you have carefully guarded the enjoyment of the poor, you will find them the most important of contributors.

The one emotion that can make you appear in the most unsympathetic light, obviously, is anger. The late Senator Joseph McCarthy—putting aside questions of right or wrong for the moment —did himself a great disservice by the vengeful, spiteful tone in which he delivered many of his public addresses. Who will ever forget those narrow eyes, the threatening manner, the cold sneer? Most people are put off by angry rhetoric. McCarthy was a verbal bully. His essential boorishness in time became apparent even to many in his own political camp. It led to his downfall. There are always a few people of an essentially fascistic bent who will respond with cheers to such rhetoric, but you will win more adherents to your cause, whatever it might be, if you come across as personally likable.

Be Yourself

These two words, good advice under almost any circumstances, are crucial in the context of public speaking. If you simply never say witty things or tell funny stories off the platform, then don't try it on the platform. It won't be natural; it won't be you.

Don't make the mistake of trying to speak the lingo of your audience if it's foreign to you. If you're over forty and addressing college-age people, for example, it's almost invariably a mistake to use young people's slang. For one thing, it can sound condescending if you don't strike just the right note. It's more likely to make you sound a bit phony and goofy, something to which young audiences are particularly sensitive. This is especially true if you are a person whose position in life carries a certain amount of natural authority and dignity. If you are a political figure, for example, a business executive, or a prominent physician or lawyer, your audiences will expect you to behave like one. Far from ingratiating yourself by pretending to be hip, you will make yourself sound even more square than you are.

For some reason that has never been clear to me, today's young people—those under thirty—incorporate more vulgarity and foul language into their everyday conversation than I would have heard in the old days outside an army barracks, garage, or waterfront saloon. Even young women use words like *pissed off*, *asshole*, and *shit* with perfectly straight faces. Perhaps they are expressing some sort of contempt for themselves and their associates by doing so, although the situation is complex. But don't do it on the speaker's platform. Even if every individual in the audience speaks that way on the street, he or she still doesn't want to hear it from the lecture platform. Since circumstances alter cases, there may be extremely rare and dramatic circumstances where such overheated language has a place. But no one will ever miss such words, even in situations of that sort, whereas people will object strongly if you use such language in most situations.

Another benefit of being yourself, speaking in a natural manner, is that audiences will be fully sympathetic—once they decide they like you—if you do happen to tip over a glass of water, cough, sneeze, or get the sniffles.

I once delivered a talk while suffering from a bad cold. At one point I simply had to say, "Ladies and gentlemen, if you'll forgive me, I'm suffering from quite a heavy cold and—believe it or not— I'm just going to have to stop here for a moment and blow my nose. If you'll excuse me—"

I turned away, blew my nose vigorously, and then got back to work.

There was no reaction at all except a slight sympathetic chuckle. If anything, the circumstance probably heightened the audience's attention in that it made them perceive me as a human being and not just a "famous entertainer" or an impersonal speaker.

Modifying Your Basic Speech for the Occasion

All politicians and office-seekers learn from experience, early in the
game, that it simply does not make sense to deliver precisely the
same speech to every audience. Most politicians do have what is
often called, around their offices, "the speech," but they also have
the sense to know that it must be modified to suit the specific needs
of separate audiences. An audience of college students, for example,
will have interests markedly different from those of an audience of
senior citizens. A witticism that might be right for a Jewish audience
may be wrong if you are speaking to a group of Chinese. An audience
consisting largely of fundamentalist Christians might be deeply moved
by a quotation from the Bible, whereas an assemblage of Unitarians
or Rationalists might be less favorably impressed.

On the subject of the practice of repeating the same speech, the
story is told of the late Maurice Francis Egan who, when he was
United States minister to Copenhagen, made a practice of visiting
the provinces of Denmark once a year to lecture on the subject of
American literature. One evening, when the king and queen of that
nation were dining at the United States legation, His Majesty said
to Egan, "We receive agreeable reports of your lectures in the
provinces. Tell me, do you use a different lecture every time?"

"No, I always use the same one, Your Majesty," Egan answered.

"But what do you do if people come a second time?"

"They never come a second time," said Egan.

Getting Off Early or Late

Many an otherwise well-constructed lecture or nightclub act has
left an audience dissatisfied after the final curtain because the speaker
or entertainer didn't know quite how—and *when*—to get off. Singers
and comedians generally learn (within a fairly short time) from
experience how to deal with this problem. It can be more troublesome to lecturers. Remember that such applause as you may receive
will rise immediately out of your closing remarks. If you just ramble
a bit at the end and suddenly stop talking, rather than reaching a
dramatic or at least an interesting conclusion, the last impression

you leave may not do justice to the earlier portions of your address. The time to give thought to this problem, of course, is not the night of your speech but the very first moment you sit down to draw up your notes or outline.

One way to finish a speech is to give a quick digest-review of it, to summarize its chief points. However, unless your remarks dealt with technical or instructional material, that will probably not be the ideal solution. You will be better advised to either restate the theme of your talk in some direct and simple way or else to conclude with the same sort of attention-getting device you employed at the beginning. In any event, keep in mind the show-business adage on the advisability of getting off "too soon," or always leaving the audience wanting more.

How Long Must You Speak to Be Effective?

It would be fortunate if I could suggest an ideal length of time for a speech—ten minutes, thirty minutes, or whatever—but it's not that simple. A gifted speaker, dealing with an inherently fascinating subject, can keep an audience transfixed for an hour or more. But such decisions should always be made in a specific context. If you're one of fourteen speakers on a program, it's obvious that no one is going to want you to run on at great length, no matter how polished an orator you are.

Even if you're the only speaker you must consider a number of factors in deciding how long your speech should run. If there is nothing much to the program except your talk, this naturally requires you to deliver a somewhat lengthy address. If, on the other hand, there are a great many components to the program, then there will be less time available for you. At some public functions, for example, there might be the following program components:

1. a cocktail hour
2. a formal welcome by the master of ceremonies
3. the pledge of allegiance to the flag
4. an invocation
5. the serving of dinner

6. the introduction of dignitaries seated at the dais or in the audience

7. brief talks by local officials or distinguished guests

8. the announcement of raffle winners and the presentation of door prizes

9. musical or variety entertainment

As you can see, two or three hours of such proceedings do not exactly prepare an audience for a lengthy address, even if the speaker is the President of the United States. The guest, in such situations, is most effective if he or she speaks for no more than thirty minutes. Many in the audience will be grateful if the speaker limits his or her time to a quarter of an hour.

The situation will, of course, be different if you are lecturing on a particular subject in which a given audience has a special interest. If you have been invited to speak on the subject of birth control, abortion, capital punishment, foreign policy, the energy crisis, or a similar sort of topic, the very fact that your audience is eager to be enlightened on the issue makes it reasonable to deliver a longer talk. In such situations a ten-minute address which might be perfectly suitable in other contexts will leave your audience disappointed.

Whatever the case, since you will have become aware of the type and length of speech expected, you will have prepared your written remarks in such a way that the number of typed pages relates to the amount of time allotted to you. It makes no sense to write a twenty-seven-page address if you have been limited to five minutes of delivery. You should, therefore, determine your approximate minutes-per-page rate of speaking.

To do so is an easy matter. You simply read three pages aloud, at the approximate pace at which you will talk when confronted with an audience, and time yourself. If, for example, reading the three pages takes six minutes, then you are devoting two minutes to the reading of each page. Once you know your minutes-per-page rate you can relate it to an address of any length.

Your timing problems are not over, however, because there are factors in speaking before a live audience that are not present when you time your speech in private. Nervousness may cause you to change your pace, or you may be interrupted—by applause if you are very fortunate, or by heckling if you are not.

Even if nothing of this sort happens, very few people are able to estimate time accurately in the absence of such clues as sunrises or sunsets. Even if you are fairly good at it, your modest ability will almost certainly evaporate once you begin a speech which requires you to concentrate on what you're saying and how you're saying it. If you've been instructed or requested to speak for a certain number of minutes, therefore, consult your watch just before you begin to speak, and glance at it once or twice during the course of your talk. Otherwise, with the best of intentions you might take a great deal more than your allotted time.

Although this might not seem like a catastrophe, it can easily become one if the program consists of more than one speaker. If there are, for instance, ten speakers and each one runs only ten minutes too long, nearly two hours have been added to the overall length of the program. Consequently, when the final speaker—who is often the featured guest of the evening—reaches the podium, the audience is in no mood to do anything but go home to bed.

A story has been told of the late Judge Vincent, one of several speakers on a banquet program years ago in Chicago. Although he had expected to be called upon shortly after eleven, it was almost two o'clock in the morning when the poor man's turn came. The toastmaster, the late Mayor Moses Handy, is reported to have introduced his Honor as follows:

"And now we come to the final speaker on this remarkable program. I would be only too happy to give him the laudatory introduction he so richly deserves, but because of the lateness of the hour, I do not wish to deprive the speaker of one moment of his allotted time, nor the ladies and gentlemen in the audience of a moment of their enjoyment. I shall therefore content myself with saying that Judge Vincent will now give his address."

The Judge arose and said, "My address is 2137 Calumet Avenue. Thank you and good night."

That the modern American attention span is shorter than ever is common enough knowledge. But perhaps we do not appreciate just how far we have fallen on this particular scale. A century ago British Prime Minister William Gladstone, noted for his rich eloquence, once addressed the House of Commons for over three hours; the attention of his listeners did not flag. His subject? The English budget of 1853! In the modern age Fidel Castro, it is said, may speak for two hours, but perhaps some of his audiences are captive.

For an example of a speech which was short but made its point, I quote here my remarks at a 1980 dinner in Los Angeles, held under the auspices of the American Civil Liberties Union. Lily Tomlin made an appearance, as did cartoonist Gary Trudeau, comedian George Carlin, Jane Pauley of the *Today* show, television producer Bud Yorkin, and a number of other dignitaries. As the name of the ACLU suggests, that organization is concerned with the preservation of American freedoms. The evening was successful, but it occurred to me that it might be a suitable occasion to express a few thoughts that, though not exactly reservations about freedom, were designed nevertheless to suggest that, in addition to supporting liberty, we ought also to look beyond that support to the likely consequences of certain efforts that are, in themselves, admirable and necessary. What follows is a transcript of partly spontaneous, partly prepared observations. (To save space I've deleted a few paragraphs.)

Some Unromantic Thoughts on Freedom

We have heard discussed this evening the politics of humor, and the humor of politics. But behind the playfulness there are, of course, serious enough realities. Comedy is, after all, about tragedy, which is to say that the raw material of most humor is essentially tragic.

As for freedom, there is a tendency to think of it in an almost material sense. We say that freedom can be won, or lost, as if there were an assured permanence to such victories or defeats.

In reality freedom cannot possibly be achieved for all time, or stockpiled, in any sense.

Freedom involves the learning of a lesson, and just as each individual has to learn for himself the basic rudiments of education—how to spell, how to read, how to count, how to think—so each of us has to learn how to be free.

A second sort of mistake in thinking about freedom is that it is a matter that is at least relatively simple; difficult, no doubt, to achieve, but not especially complex inherently.

In fact there is an incredible complexity to freedom.

The choice is not simply between total, beautiful freedom on the one hand and cruel tyranny on the other. If the choice were so simple, who would choose tyranny? The word for total freedom—by the way—is anarchy, which has never been popular or even possible. In the world of reality, looking at the whole planet and a long expanse of time, we see that, for all its unpopularity in the context of American experience, tyranny is nevertheless the norm and freedom the relatively rare exception.

There is a tragic element in the achievement of freedom, so that even the infrequent moments of victory for its supporters are touched with ambiguity as well as new insights into the unavoidable imperfections that characterize the human predicament.

For it is not the case that freedom's only enemy is tyranny.

One freedom—as it happens—may be opposed by another.

Another tragic component of the achievement of freedom is that its fruits are by no means always noble, edifying, or socially constructive.

Unknown millions of heretics, martyrs, freethinkers, and dissenters died in the long, bloody campaign to achieve freedom of religion. And one result of that freedom was enacted recently in Guyana.

Countless heroes have distinguished themselves in the long struggle for the freedom to publish, and among the results of their glorious victory is the publication of psychotic Nazi literature, periodicals specializing in child pornography, and magazines like *Hustler*, which—as various women's groups have pointed out—are an insult to women.

Today's pornography, as feminist Robin Morgan has written, "promulgates rape, mutilation, and even murder as average sexual acts, depicting the normal man as a sadist and the healthy woman as a willing victim."

Norman Cousins has said, "In our own business—books and magazines—we are often astonished to see what passes for triumphant achievement in the cause of freedom. A writer we know exulted because he was able to get a half-dozen four-letter words past an editor who may well have been elated because he was able to get the same words into print past his editorial chief. At one time in the history of publishing, freedom was connected to things worth saying. Writers like Ida Tarbell, Lincoln Steffens, and Walter Lippmann saw a connection between freedom to print and the need to do battle with predatory forces in the society. There is nothing wrong with the four-letter word per se; what is wrong is the disfiguration of values that makes the four-letter word a symbol of literary freedom and excellence."

Supporters of this admirable organization [the ACLU] do not have to be told of the difficult struggle to restrain abuses of police authority, and to set reasonable limits to it.

But one result of that achievement of freedom is that notorious professional criminals, narcotics wholesalers, and violent thugs of various sorts occasionally escape punishment when everyone knowledgeable about their cases is perfectly aware of their guilt.

Those of us who support the right of the American working man to organize in defense of his interests have welcomed news of the successes of such heroic figures as César Chávez, among many who might be mentioned.

But such hard-won freedom has also resulted in the assumption of massive social power by the Mafia murderers who infest certain unions, and by such disgraces to the labor movement as the leadership of the Teamsters Union. (I speak, incidentally, only for myself here, not for the ACLU.)

Those of us with even a casual familiarity with history are aware of the incredible obstacles that had to be surmounted before democratic institutions could be established. We know that democracy failed in its birthplace—ancient Athens—and that it was a long time before it was given another chance.

In time—in this nation, among others—we won this additional freedom—the freedom to vote, to at least participate in the making of political decisions. We use the phrase *the people* in a sort of romantic, idealistic sense. And indeed there are few political dramas more inspiring than those in which an informed, committed populace asserts its rights and exercises them responsibly.

But, having achieved this additional victory, we now are dismayed as we look back to survey the battleground, which we thought had been pacified. For the power of the people—it turns out—may lead to tyranny just as may the power of king, dictator, aristocracy, or party.

We had assumed that, because there are buildings called schools, those who came out of them at the end of some sort of educative process automatically constituted an informed and socially sensitive electorate. Not to mention those who don't go to the schools at all, or don't go long enough even to learn to read above the fourth- or fifth-grade level.

But we have seen poll after poll confirm the unhappy fact that if the Bill of Rights were submitted to "the people" now, it would by no means necessarily be supported, either at all or in its present form.

On the stage of world affairs the present prospects for democracy are dim and getting dimmer. The United Nations now consists of over 140 nations. Only a handful of them are real democracies.

As for our own international activities, we have perceived many of them (and quite rightly, as it happens; Stalin was indeed a moral monster) as involving a *defense* of freedom.

But this virtuous ideal resulted in our forming alliances with any military dictatorship that shared our contempt for a common enemy, so that in seeking to defend freedom we have, in some times and places, diminished freedom.

Well, until just a few hours ago I had assumed—in fact, planned—that my participation in this evening's proceedings would be simply to master such ceremonies as I could, perhaps get a laugh or two, and tomorrow morning send another check to the ACLU.

But late this afternoon I found myself drawn to my typewriter, where these few gloomy observations were produced.

What have I been saying? Actually it's a modest enough assertion, that in the defense of freedom we should not think of it as do schoolchildren or Kiwanis lecturers, which is to say romantically or naively. Nor as do certain right-wing polemicists, to whom freedom may mean chiefly getting government agencies off their backs so they can make more money by taking advantage of their employees or customers.

No, the whole picture is—as I've said—incredibly complex.

To deal rationally with that complexity we must certainly first acknowledge its existence.

Not everyone present that evening wanted to hear that sort of message—which leads us to an important subject: audiences and their effect on your presentation.

Your Audience

An Audience Is One Entity

Audiences have always fascinated me. The most interesting thing about them is that each one has a single definite character. Although it may be comprised of a thousand individuals, an audience has one personality. Perhaps it is this fact that makes it easy for demagogues and dictators to control large masses of people; they are really not controlling a million entities, just one.

Part of my business is to work with individuals to create humor out of thin air. But for an appreciation of this humor and a reaction to it, I am at the mercy of that "big, black giant," the audience in toto.

Another thing you ought to know about audiences is that should you lecture every night for the next century, you will never run into any two identical in their reactions.

For some audiences you can do no wrong. With others you can, seemingly, do nothing right, even though you personally are a common factor and are performing just as well on the one occasion as on the other. It is chiefly comedians, however, who suffer the pains and enjoy the blessings of such differences. Reactions to speakers are not ordinarily so dramatic.

Producers, critics, and sponsors, of course, are weary of hearing comedians complain about bad audiences. "Every time Milton Berle has a bad show," a writer I know once said to me, "he blames it on his audience."

If the report is true, Milton is right more often than wrong. An audience can be either good or bad before the curtain goes up, before the performer can have had any effect on it. If an audience is really unprepared to receive a particular bit of entertainment, not all the brilliance in the world can salvage the day. I first became aware of this phenomenon while working at CBS on the West Coat in the late 1940s, when it was my custom to peek around the curtain each evening before I walked on stage to begin the program. I soon discovered that there were three different kinds of audiences.

The first was the average expectant but calm assemblage, and when I turned in a poor performance in front of such a group I had no one to blame but myself.

The second kind was the good audience. A glance from the wings would reveal a crowd rippling with carnival atmosphere, laughing, craning necks, whispering, talking, making a great deal of noise, ready to have a good time no matter what. And no matter what, they did. They would greet my weakest quip with a mighty roar of approval. The man who could function before such mobs day in and day out could rule the world.

Then there would be the occasional bad audience. Looking from behind the curtain one might think they had come to attend a funeral. There would be no laughter, no talk—just polite, resigned attention. All viewers in the theater looked as if they had just finished arguing with their spouses. They sat silently and listlessly, again before the curtain had gone up and before the performer could have been held responsible in any way for the crowd's mood.

For years I have conducted a haphazard sort of research into what mysterious factors so clearly determine the character of an audience the moment it has come in off the street (or even before). For a time I thought it was something as simple as rainy weather, but I soon discovered that reaction on one rainy night would be wonderful, but disastrous on the next. Then I considered the national or local emotional climate as dictated by important news events of the day, but was eventually obliged to discard that possibility too.

Some say, "I'll bet it's nothing more than the day of the week. Good shows on Saturday when people are out to have a high time and bad shows on Monday when they're feeling let down after the weekend." The hypothesis doesn't hold up. Certainly Saturday night is usually a big night in the theater, but taking this into account obviously doesn't explain why every so often there's a slow Saturday or a lively Monday.

I finally pinned down a secondary reason for the moodiness of audiences: air conditioning and room temperature. Often an out-of-whack air conditioning system makes an audience hot, restless, and preoccupied with its own discomfort. This is an obstacle the entertainer or lecturer sometimes has to surmount, but just when I thought I had discovered ingredient X, I found out there were too many exceptions: good shows on hot, sticky nights and bad shows on comfortable evenings.

Currently I am of the opinion that changes in the atmospheric pressure, sunspots, moon phases, cosmic radiation, or something of that sort may be responsible. Statistics show that suicides do not occur in equal numbers every day but cluster in certain peak periods.

We are all familiar with days when things just get off to a bad start and stay that way; frequently we learn that we are not alone in feeling out of sorts. Many investigators feel that sudden changes in atmospheric pressure may have peculiar and as yet little-understood effects on our emotional or glandular equipment. I leave it to authorities to prove or disprove my thoeries, but in passing submit the following bit of evidence.

On some nights things are bad all over town. Performers in one play will complain or enthuse about an audience only to discover that players in another company share their sentiments. Jayne used to report that the fans at her *I've Got a Secret* panel show were especially receptive on the same evening that I had a good audience. David Wayne and Tom Ewell, two of Broadway's most popular leading men, decided to put this actor's theory to a test some years ago when they were appearing in *Teahouse of the August Moon* and *Seven Year Itch*, respectively. Each evening after the final curtain they would compare notes by telephone on audience response. They discovered that their audiences were identical in mood far more often than mere chance would have allowed. Obviously something external was responsible.

Pay Attention to Your Audience

External factors aside, it is a speaker's responsibility to be sensitive to his or her audience. Nobody likes the man or woman who totally dominates a conversation, constantly interrupts, and engages chiefly in monologue rather than dialogue. A speech, obviously enough, is a monologue, although it may adopt other forms during formal debates or question-and-answer periods. But even when you are doing all the talking, you will still be well advised to attend to the responses your audience makes.

If you're not sure about the bias and emotions of your audience, just listen to its responses. While making a campaign speech, a candidate for political office sought to discover the denominational sympathies of his audience. "My great-grandfather," he began, "was an Episcopalian [stony silence], but my great-grandmother belonged to the Congregational Church [continued silence]. My grandfather was a Baptist [more silence], while my grandmother was a Presbyterian [still frigid silence]. But I had a great-aunt who was a Methodist [loud applause]. And I have always followed my great-aunt [loud and continued cheering]." He was elected.

The point is a simple one: On most occasions it will be to your advantage to know how your audience feels about the subject you may be speaking on. Obviously, this won't apply if you're speaking to the Garden Club on the care and feeding of rhododendrons. But if your subject matter has even a hint of controversy about it, you would do well to know, if only so that you are braced for it, what the audience's reactions might be. You need not ingratiate yourself with them if that is not your purpose, but you should know where you stand.

On extremely rare occasions you will not be able to miss a negative response because it may take the form of cries of "You dirty Communist!" or a mass exodus or a tomato flung at you. Far more likely, fortunately, will be positive reactions such as attentive half-smiles, expressions of concentrated attention, laughter, applause, and even—on rare occasions—cheers. But there are other, more common and subtle reactions of which you should be aware: occasional waves of coughing, low-level whispering, or muttering. Such distractions are clues that reveal how an audience is receiving your performance.

If an outbreak of restlessness occurs—as evidenced by coughing or whispering—it is a certain indication that something has gone wrong. If at such a moment you had intended to speak for another fifteen minutes you would be well advised to throw this part of the plan overboard at once and bring your address to as graceful a conclusion as possible.

You will ordinarily receive a smattering of polite applause when you are introduced. You are fortunate if it lasts as long as it takes to walk from your chair to the microphone or lectern. Whether you are totally unknown or a figure of world prominence, you always feel a bit disconcerted if the applause stops before you reach your target area. Walking those last few seconds in silence does little to inflate your confidence, so don't dawdle.

At the close of your address the audience will advise you, generally by the volume of applause, as to what sort of job you did.

You need only smile and nod a thank-you by way of gracious response. In the unlikely event that the applause persists or amounts to an ovation, you must then, of course, rise and express your appreciation more openly. Do not, under any circumstances, be tempted to return to the podium for an encore. Entertainers sometimes do, but not speakers.

Although you should direct almost all of your concentrated attention to the task of the moment, do—I repeat—reserve a bit of it for your audience. It is your hearers who will decide—as you go along—how well or poorly you are doing. There's no point at all to feeling that they are simply insensitive boors if they indicate that they are not favorably impressed by your remarks. Inasmuch as your purpose was to affect them, it logically follows that if they believe you have failed, then you have and that's all there is to it.

Do not be discouraged, however, if such an unhappy situation arises. There will be other audiences and speeches. No doubt on some future occasion your wisdom and charm will be more warmly appreciated. And be assured that the vast majority of your audiences will be polite to you and receptive to your presentation.

Chapter 6

The Ad-Lib
Speech

Some speakers prefer to address audiences on an extemporaneous basis. They feel restricted by a prewritten text and may be somewhat stilted in reading it. Others, as we have seen, are just the opposite: They are quite comfortable when given the security of a prepared address and petrified at the thought of having to walk out on stage with their hands in their pockets and nothing on paper. Actually, extemporaneous speechmaking is the easiest thing in the world so long as one particular factor is attended to: *knowledge of the territory*.

If you are, let us say, a garage machanic, you could presumably give a twelve-hour lecture on the subject of automobile engines, speaking out of nothing more than your experience and practical knowledge. But if you were asked to give a speech on brain surgery you wouldn't be able to say much at all. If you want to speak off the cuff, therefore, be sure you know what you're talking about. If you do, just relax and let it flow.

Although the news may come as a surprise, you already know how to ad-lib. As a matter of fact, you've been doing it every day of your life since you were about two years old. Even now when you go into, say, a meat market, nobody hands you a script. You simply go up to the butcher and tell him what you want. When you go to a barber you're never the least bit at a loss for words; you just give him the necessary instructions. The world does not place a fresh scenario at your bedside every morning as you get up and prepare to go about your duties. You simply say whatever you want to say, and that's all there is to the matter.

When you consider speaking extemporaneously on a lecture platform, therefore, be comforted by the knowledge that you may have had thirty or forty years' experience at the very task you are about to undertake. The human memory being remarkably sieve-like, however, you will be even more comfortable if you provide yourself with the memory aid of a few notes.

Although I am one of that small fraternity of comedians who actually ad-lib fresh material—jokes appropriate to a particular occasion and unlikely, therefore, ever to be heard again—the fact is that a good many of the things I say as an after-dinner speaker occur to me during the hour or so before I get up to address the audience. I generally make notes throughout the evening, starting not just with the formal program but with my entry into the room. Almost invariably there is something that catches my attention or strikes me as odd or funny. It may be the wallpaper, a chandelier with three of its bulbs burned out, an orchestra playing disco music when the average age of the audience is sixty-five, or a tray of dishes spilled by a waiter.

To give an example from recent experience, I had the pleasure not long ago of flying to Scottsdale, Arizona, to take part in a retirement party honoring a friend from high school named Ted Edmundson. One of the first speakers of the evening was Judge Ogg, today an important Arizona jurist but originally just a first-grade school friend of Ted's. He mentioned that Edmundson—among other things a musician—had acquired his first guitar because Ogg, who is left-handed, had been given a right-handed guitar by his mother. Since he couldn't use it, he traded it to Ted "for three horny-toads."

When—about an hour later—it was my turn to address the audience, I said, "I was interested to hear Judge Ogg relate the story of how Ted happened to acquire his first guitar. And it's quite an interesting story, too, because to this day Ted plays very good horny-toad."

Hardly a joke to be ranked with the best or even worst of Mark Twain, Voltaire, or Oscar Wilde, but it was perfectly appropriate to the moment, as were the other witticisms that had occurred to me during the earlier part of the evening.

Even if you are the only speaker at a civic function, and assuming you have an adequate grasp of the subject matter you'll be talking about, it will still be a good idea to have in your pocket a card or piece of paper listing the several points you want to bring out. You can give a perfectly effective talk without such a memory aid, but if you do there's always the chance that, on the way home, you will suddenly slap your forehead and say "Damn! I forgot to mention the most important thing of all."

A gifted speaker who was not above resorting to tricks of the trade was the late Mayor James "Jimmy" Walker of New York.

A journalist once saw Walker impress an audience by saying, "Ladies and gentlemen, I arrived here this evening with some written remarks, but I've decided to discard my prepared speech and just speak to you from the heart." With that, Walker crumpled a page he had been carrying, tossed it aside, and delivered a fiery and effective address. At the close of the evening's proceedings the journalist picked up the discarded page and looked at it. The piece of paper was simply a printed advertisement. Walker had prepared no remarks at all for the occasion. He did not need to; like many practiced speakers, he simply delivered a talk consisting largely of things he had said many times before.

Tips for Effective Ad-Lib Speaking

Don't Digress

You should become consciously aware of the degree to which you tend to digress in normal communication, because this may happen if you are speaking extemporaneously. Very few people are able to totally resist the temptation to get off the track. Ordinarily this is not a serious failing, but there are situations where it can be disastrous. If, for example, you are on duty at an emergency hotline crisis center and someone calls to report an accident, you will want the caller to be brief and to the point. You would hardly welcome a message delivered as follows:

> I'm calling to tell you people about a serious accident, and I hope you do a better job of taking care of the matter this time than you did the last time I called you. I think it was five—no, maybe it was more like six or seven weeks ago—anyway, I called one time and the first thing that went wrong was the phone rang for about a minute before anybody picked it up. And when somebody did answer, they were sort of rude to me, if you don't mind my saying so. Anyway, what I'm calling you about this time is that—

It does not require a great deal of imagination to perceive that a life might literally be lost if a caller were to so ramble.

Oddly enough, it is not just stupid people who do this. I know some individuals whose very intelligence and creative ability get in the way of their delivering a simple message. One friend in particular tends to communicate as follows:

> You really ought to see the darling suit I got yesterday when I was— No, I'm wrong. It wasn't yesterday; it was Saturday. I'm sure it was Saturday because I can remember saying to our housekeeper, "Now, Bessie, I can't drive you home until noon, because Bob is out jogging and he won't be back with the car until then." Saturday is Bob's jogging day, you know. Incidentally, you ought to see him. Jogging has been so wonderful for him that he's taken off over twenty pounds and he looks ten years younger. Of course, I suppose the fact that he touches up his hair a bit helps, but I think it's just marvelous. I think a man *ought* to look young as long as he can, don't you?

At about this time one tends to remind the woman that she started to talk about the purchase of a new suit.

That habit of digressing can be, in an otherwise charming person, moderately endearing, and it can be amusing if encountered in the make-believe context of a situation-comedy television program, but it's a poor way to run a railroad if your purpose is to communicate intelligibly with an audience. You should, therefore, get the general thrust of your message clear in your own mind. The individual components should be sharply focused, too. Don't lose sight of the main purpose of your communication as you deliver your remarks.

A good speech, you see, has an essential unity. This is not to say that no digressions are permitted, but they ought not to be uncontrolled and rambling. They must always have relevance that is either obvious or quickly explained.

Know the Territory

Because the point is so important, let's go over it again.

If you are going to give an ad-lib speech, be sure you thoroughly know the subject matter on which you will be speaking. There are two ways to know the territory: by experience and by research. If Tommy Lasorda, manager of the Los Angeles Dodgers, is called upon to give a speech on baseball, he need only refer to his vast store of information on the subject. You and I, if lecturing on the same subject, would have to gather information by interviewing players or team executives, studying the sports page, reading books about baseball, and so on.

Speak in Sentences

Although the news may come as a shock to you, you should know that you are alive in a period of American history, and present in an environment, in which speaking in actual sentences has become something of a lost art. You may imagine that you speak almost entirely in sentences. The fact is that you almost certainly do not. If you did you would be unlikely to have consulted a book such as this. To illustrate the point, I'll state a simple message in grammatically acceptable form and then show how the same idea might be conveyed by the average American.

First, the message:

> We are alive today at a dangerous point in our nation's history. The list of problems that perplex us is depressing by its very length, and the individual problems themselves, we now recognize, are incredibly complex.

Quite a simple point. But the average person would express it more or less as follows:

> There are a lot of—uh—a lot of very difficult—uh—you know, really tough problems that we face—these days, I mean. Maybe things are worse than—uh—worse than they ever were when—uh—There's a lot—there *are* a lot of problems, and I don't think that—you know, either us or the President or anybody understands them or—uh—knows, when you get right down to it, I mean, exactly what's the—I mean what should be done about a lot of the—you know—uh—like, things that make up the problems.

This is no exaggeration. I'm not suggesting that college presidents or U.S. senators express themselves so ineptly, but there are very few college presidents and senators. The next time you see a TV newscaster in the parking lot of a supermarket, at a busy intersection, or on a university campus, soliciting opinions from passersby on some important social question, pay careful attention to the thought processes and sentence structure of those who give their views. It would surely depress the Founding Fathers if they could hear it. It depresses me.

You may be one of the fortunate few who have the gift of easy, lucid, and at least mostly grammatical expression, but the statistical chances are against it. Perhaps it doesn't matter all that much in your home or down at the corner bar, but it will matter a great deal indeed on the lecture platform. Audiences will tolerate a certain amount of incoherence, but it will have to be kept to a minimum.

It may occur to you that you will simply never get to the point where you can make a speech without note cards or a typed page in front of you. So what? As mentioned earlier, Ronald Reagan for years made the same speech, with slight variations, and always with a well-worn stack of hand-printed note cards in front of him. Reagan's previous profession was that of radio announcer and actor, of course, so it's understandable that he would be accustomed to using scripts, cue cards, and other people's ideas. But the point is that if the President can't ad-lib a good speech, why should you worry about your inability to do so? Stick to cards, notes, or a typed text if you are more comfortable doing so.

Extemporizing During a Question Period

Your answers to unexpected questions, of course, will be extemporaneous, so be sure to have an understanding with your hosts—long before you are introduced—as to whether time should be allotted for questions and answers and, if so, how much. If you're new to the speechmaking business, you might not want to tackle this on your first few times out, although if you happen to be well informed on the subject matter it should be no serious problem.

The makeup of the audience is an important factor. If you are, for instance, a dentist, you could obviously spend hours answering questions from people whose only qualification to interrogate you is that they have teeth. If you're that same dentist and your audience consists of instructors at a dental school, you probably won't want to have to answer any questions at all.

If you and the host group do agree that a question-and-answer period should be included, then you face the decision as to whether you will entertain written or spoken questions. There's no right or wrong to this. Questions from the floor are generally easy to deal with in a small room, but impossible to accommodate in most large auditoriums, for obvious reasons. For one thing, the audience must be able to hear the questioners, and since they usually don't have microphones their voices are simply lost in large halls. Sometimes this problem is dealt with by having the speaker repeat the questions, but this can be time-consuming and annoying.

When it is necessary, because of the size of the room, to repeat questions, it is not absolutely required that your repetition be word for word. Since some who put questions are not practiced at public speaking, they may ramble, digress, or otherwise obscure their points. In such cases you should simply state the essence of the question as quickly and concisely as possible.

It may even be to your interest to deliberately revise the wording of the question in such a way as to clarify it or to make it easier to answer or to make a joke about. Some years ago when I was entertaining questions from an audience in a television studio, a woman asked, "When will this program be aired?"

"Well," I said, "first it will be fumigated; then—"

Because the response got a good laugh, it remained in my mental computer. A year or so later a man in the audience asked, "When will this program be telecast?"

"You mean when will it be aired?" I replied.

"Yes," he said.

At which I repeated the original ad-lib.

In some auditoriums there may be reason to be concerned about hecklers or nuts and kooks. Such considerations may necessitate that all questions be written and submitted during the program.

Again, if you're well informed on the subject matter of your talk, you can handily deal with questions you haven't anticipated. Obviously, it's easier still if you have the opportunity to see them prior to the time for your response. If there is a dinner connected with the event, there will be ample time for the question cards to be gathered and brought to you. You may wish to have the questions read aloud by the master or mistress of ceremonies, or you may prefer to read them yourself.

Almost invariably a question or two will come up that you are not adequately prepared, at the moment, to answer. It's much better to concede your predicament at once, in a simple, straightforward manner, rather than trying to fake and bumble your way through a response, pretending to knowledge that you don't have.

Although it will occasionally be necessary to give a full, detailed response to a question, you should as a rule try to keep answers brief and precise. One reason is that not everyone in the audience will share the questioner's interest in the particular aspect of the larger subject that he or she has brought up. Another is that quite a number of people may be waiting their turn to pose questions. If you spend too much time on one or more of them, you make it less likely that others will have the opportunity to participate. The late President John Kennedy was a master at this sort of thing. Politicians generally are better at it than the rest of us, although it's true that they sometimes give a short answer because that represents all they know on the question at hand. Lastly, a short, well-thought-out answer is easier to understand and retain than a long, rambling response.

Don't be afraid, by the way, to express your personal feelings during the question-and-answer period. Obviously the question itself may dictate the form of your answer. If someone asks you what is the capitol of Wyoming you simply give them the information and get on to a more meaningful question. But in most cases the questioners request your opinion rather than factual information. They may say, "Do you think the experience of modern China holds any lessons for Americans?" "What can I, as a parent, do about the problems of drug abuse?" Most questions you hear will be of this general sort.

You may, if you wish, be gracious enough to refer to opinions that differ with your own. You might say, "Well, the President of the United States wouldn't agree with me about this, but I feel . . ." Or, "Most of you here this evening who are over fifty years old may not see it the same way, but in my view . . ."

Don't be afraid of responding to questions. For me, it's the most stimulating aspect of public speaking.

Chapter 7

Should You Employ Humor?

You might give a moment's reflection to why humor can be such an effective device for a speaker. It accomplishes two things: It puts the audience at ease, and it makes your listeners more favorably disposed toward you. Even if a given audience might have some reason for being less than sympathetic (suppose you're affiliated with a rival political party, represent a racial or religious minority, or are known to hold an unpopular opinion), the successful telling of a joke or amusing story communicates to the audience that you're not such a bad fellow after all.

In considering whether or not you should use humor, do not make the mistake of thinking of humor as one thing. It is not *a* thing at all. It is a word that can be applied to many different forms of expression. You might suppose that professional comedians could employ any form of the art for their purposes. In fact, this is not the case. The reasons you laugh at Bob Newhart are quite different from those that made you laugh at Groucho Marx. There's very little in common between the humor of Steve Martin and that of Art Buchwald.

Assuming that you're a nonprofessional, you will probably want to employ only three types of humor: (*a*) the brief joke, (*b*) the funny story, or (*c*) something based on personal experience, not necessarily your own. Perhaps you have already decided which of these forms is best for you in that it is the type you most frequently employ in normal conversation. Do you make your friends laugh with silly lines, little jokes, plays on words? The same approach will probably work for you on the lecture platform. Are you most amusing when telling a story about something that actually happened to you, or are you better at telling funny stories of the conventional two-Irishmen-got-off-a-streetcar type? In general it makes sense to work from your own natural strengths, whether you are preparing a lecture or, for that matter, doing almost anything in life.

The employment of humor on the lecture platform, however, requires a certain delicacy of judgment. There are situations where it shouldn't be used at all. And when it is, there must always be some relevance between the joke, your purpose of the moment, and the interests of the audience. It would obviously be unwise to do jokes about cocaine and extramarital sex if you're addressing an audience in a church hall, or to do jokes about barnyard animals if you're speaking to a sophisticated urban group.

Again, be extremely careful about vulgar, off-color humor. It isn't that such jokes won't get a laugh; they usually will. Even when they are utterly inappropriate to the occasion there will almost always be a few insensitive clods who will respond with laughter—but there's a good chance that you will have offended everyone else. Even those who have laughed may not, after a moment's reflection, approve of either your joke or their own response to it. Never has anyone said to a speaker, "You gave a marvelous talk, but I wish you had told a few more dirty jokes." There have been many instances, however, when people have said, "His lecture was very interesting and entertaining. It's a shame he had to resort to off-color humor to get laughs."

Such an experienced lecturer as Art Linkletter says, "I never tell a dirty joke, or even a slightly off-color one. If there is any doubt in my mind, I discard the joke completely. What's the point of irritating even one person in a crowd that may number in the thousands? There are plenty of clean jokes, so why take a chance?"

Another thing to bear in mind is that American audiences have now been brainwashed by over thirty-five years of professional humor on television, not to mention on radio and record albums, and in films, nightclubs, and theaters. In attempting to do jokes you are, in a sense, competing with full-time practitioners of the trade. Consequently, in your first few speeches you should employ humor to a very slight degree, if at all. If all goes well, you can then, in later talks, increase the funniness component. You'll never be criticized for giving an audience "too little" humor, but you can get into dreadful trouble giving them too much.

How to Use Humor

Let's say that you do decide to experiment with a joke or two in your next talk but have a poor memory for funny stories. Where do you find material? At any bookstore or library there are dozens of joke collections available. You'll have to do quite a bit of reading to find just the right lines for your purposes, but others have already done the research for you, so you might as well take advantage of their industry.

Incidentally, you need have no moral scruples about changing names and details of funny stories to suit your purposes. Suppose you come across a story about something funny that happened twenty-five years ago in Chicago and involved three people totally unknown to you. There's nothing wrong with jokingly suggesting that it happened in your town, "just the other day," and to people with whom the audience might be familiar.

Whatever you do, don't try the joke or story in public without first working it over in private. We've already considered the importance of rehearsing your speech; the importance of rehearsing the humorous portion of it is even more acute. Remember that a speech is intended for the ear, not the eye. Consequently the wording of a story that seemed so right when you found it in a newspaper, magazine, or collection of jokes might be totally inappropriate and stilted when you deliver it from the podium.

In introducing the story try to avoid such cliches as "I'm reminded of the story about . . ." It's best just to jump right into the account without such a shopworn preamble.

If your story quotes actual or alleged conversation, it's vital that the words be those of common speech and do not sound literary or artificial. If your story involves dialogue it's best to use the simple verb *said*, whereas if the story is written it may include words such as *responded, whispered quizzically, made the rejoinder*, and so on.

If your personal gifts do not incline toward depending heavily on humor, then you would be wise to consult other works on the subject. A good one to start you off is *The Enjoyment of Laughter* by Max Eastman.

Beware of Your Own Cleverness

Some speakers are more naturally gifted at wit than others, but as in the ancient story of the tortoise and the hare, the race is not always to the swift. There are some lecturers and debaters who occasionally lose the sympathy of an audience because they are rude, too coldly witty, overbearing, or glib.

Senator Robert Dole of Kansas aroused a certain amount of resentment on the part of at least a percentage of his hearers not only when he was the Republican vice-presidential candidate under Gerald Ford, but also when he became a presidential contender himself in 1979. Dole's very gifts—a biting wit, a sharp-edged quickness of mind—lost him the sympathy of some of his audiences.

The gifted debater William F. Buckley has occasionally been similarly troubled. Bill loses some of his listeners by a tendency to use polysyllabic words when it is not necessary to do so. And he has—particularly during the early years of his career as a polemicist—sometimes been guilty of intellectual bullying, attacking his opponent in so waspish a way that, although his was the better argument as of a given moment, he nevertheless came across as unsympathetic, which in turn detracted from the appeal of his message. There is little likelihood that you need be concerned about this danger, but if you are noted as a witty and sometimes cutting conversationalist you would be well advised to give the point careful thought.

There are, of course, occasions when "good-natured kidding" of another speaker or guest is appropriate. If the event at which you're speaking has a guest of honor, and you decide to open with a humorous observation or two about her or him, you might consider doing some sort of "roast"-type joke about the honoree. Some years ago—after I had written a book called *The Funny Men*, about a dozen or so then-popular television comedians—television producer-writer Hal Kanter, one of our wittiest after-dinner speakers, "roasted" me publicly. "When the roll of the great comedians is called up yonder," said Kanter, setting up the audience to expect a compliment, "Steve Allen will be there to call the roll."

The put-down was so clever that I've never objected to it in the least—in fact, I often quote it. However, if you want to do this sort of joke about a guest of honor you must give thought to the total setting, the composition of the audience, the degree of dignity of the distinguished guest, and so forth. Also, you must adequately assess your own role in such a social drama. Hal Kanter was not being in the least offensive because it was an instance of one television humorist speaking, in good nature, about another. But if you are, let us say, merely the best insurance salesperson in Davenport, Iowa, and the guest of honor is the governor of the state, you'd better select an opening gambit of a more respectful sort.

It's also possible to say something amusing about a guest without insulting her or him. I was asked to appear at a tribute to George Gobel some time back and, since I've always liked George, accepted the invitation. Later, however, it developed that I had to work on the date of the affair, so I revised my remarks slightly and arranged to have them played in tape-recorded form.

Hi, everybody. This is— Wait a minute, I've got it here someplace. [papers rustling]

Oh, yes. Hi, everybody; this is *Annette Funicello*.

Wait a minute . . . Ah, *here* we are. Hi, everybody, this is Steve Allen.

At least, this is a tape recording of Steve Allen.

Steve Allen himself at this moment is taping a comedy special for NBC.

And if NBC has any successful comedy going at all these days, that's pretty special.

In any event at the moment I'm busily occupied explaining the jokes to Fred Silverman. Consequently I can't be in two places at once.

I could have arranged to be in three places at once but nobody asked me.

Be that as it may—and I don't think it was—I really did want to be at the Sportsmen's Lodge today because, although I have never seen an actual sportsman lodging there, I have been a lifelong fan of George Gobel.

As a matter of fact I'm probably a Gobel fan of longer standing than anyone in the room because I first listened to him when he was known as "Little Georgie Gobel," singing on the old WLS Band Dance show in Chicago back in the early 1930s.

That was actually his name. Little Georgie Gobel.

There were a lot of little people in radio in those days. There was little Jack Little.

Then there was little Mary Small.

Or was it *small* Mary *Little?*

Anyway, my family used to listen to George a lot. This was back in the wonderful days when we also listened to *Amos 'n Andy, Myrt and Marge, Lum and Abner,* and Sally and Gertrude.

You probably don't remember Sally and Gertrude, but that's perfectly understandable because they were just two young women who lived next door to me.

I used to listen to them a lot, through the wallpaper, but I never could quite make out what they were saying.

Or doing.

Anyway, those were great days for radio.

And they weren't bad days for our country either. At least you could walk the streets in safety.

Although a lot of people on those streets were keeling over from hunger because that was during the Depression.

And they didn't ask for Social Security or Welfare, either.

They did the patriotic American thing. They just lay there and starved.

But years later I was glad to find out that not only was George Gobel a good country singer but he was also very funny.

One thing I've always admired about George Gobel was that he never copied anybody else. He's always had his own original style.

Even today he's original in that he's the only person in show business who has *not* been mentioned as Johnny Carson's replacement.

Anyway, I just wanted to get on the tape machine here to say these few words about George. You notice I did not say I wanted to get "on the horn."

Because I did get on a horn one time, and it was very painful.

I'm glad you're giving praise and respect to George Gobel today—quite honestly—because he's a comedian. There are very few comedians on earth so we'd better take care of the ones we have.

Bye-bye, George.

The Human Touch of Humor

If you're a beginner at the joke-telling trade, you might want to employ an ancient device which gives you a certain amount of protection: attributing the joke—accurately or not—to some recognized and popular wit. I sometimes toy with an audience by saying, "As Mark Twain once observed"—after which I simply do a line of my own. Then, after the audience has laughed, I share with them the information that Mark Twain had nothing to do with what I just said. It might be that only a professional comedian can get away with that sort of device, but many speakers prefer to introduce a joke by saying, "That puts me in mind of a wonderful story that Danny Thomas used to tell" or "On the subject of politicians, Will Rogers once had this to say." If the jokes get big laughs you've won the point. If they get a modest response—well, it wasn't entirely your fault.

Far better than a formula joke, and even better than a funny story, is humor with the ring of truth to it. If you can relate an actual incident, whether it happened to you or to someone else, and if, furthermore, your listeners realize that they are hearing a true story, the results will almost invariably be satisfactory.

The next example provides a clear illustration of the after-dinner speaking style of one of the great lecturers of American history, Mark Twain. The time was November 1879; the place, Chicago. The Army of the Tennessee had organized a banquet for their first commander, General Ulysses S. Grant. In that day, toasts were common, and it was not unusual for a dozen or more to be offered by various speakers. One gentleman present proposed the classic toast, "To the ladies—as they comfort us in our sorrows, let us not forget them in our festivities."

The following speaker was Twain, who offered a toast "To the babies—as they comfort us in our sorrows, let us not forget them in our festivities."

After the laughter had subsided, the great humorist made some additional remarks—partly prepared, partly extemporaneous.

The style of joking in the last century was more temperate, more literary, than the Friars Roast sort of rapid-fire material common at present. Nevertheless, it is still possible—even after so long a time—to appreciate the warmth, wisdom, and good cheer of Twain's observations, which will have particular meaning for mothers and fathers.

I like that. We have not all had the good fortune to be ladies. We have not all been generals, or poets or statesmen; but when the toast works down to the babies, we stand on common ground.

It's a shame that for a thousand years the world's banquets have utterly ignored the baby, as if he didn't amount to anything. If you will stop and think a minute—if you will go back fifty or one hundred years to your early married life—and recontemplate your first baby—you will remember that he amounted to a good deal, and even something over.

You soldiers all know that when that little fellow arrived

at family headquarters you had to hand in your resignation. He took entire command.

You became his lackey, his mere body-servant, and you had to stand around, too. He was not a commander who made allowances for time, distance, weather or anything else. You had to execute his order, whether it was possible or not.

And there was only one form of marching in his manual of tactics, and that was the double-quick. He treated you with every sort of insolence and disrespect, and the bravest of you didn't dare to say a word. You could face the death-storm at Donelson and Vicksburg, and give back blow for blow; but when he clawed your whiskers, and pulled your hair, and twisted your nose, you had to take it.

When the thunders of war were sounding in your ears you set your faces toward the batteries and advanced with steady tread; but when he turned on the terrors of his war-whoop you advanced in the other direction, and mighty glad of the chance, too.

When he called for soothing-syrup, did you venture to throw out any side remarks about certain services being unbecoming an officer and a gentleman? No. You got up and got it. When he ordered his bottle and it was not warm, did you talk back? Not you. You went to work and warmed it. You even descended so far in your menial office as to take a suck at that warm, insipid stuff yourself to see if it was right—three parts water to one of milk, a touch of sugar to modify the colic, and a drop of peppermint to kill those immortal hiccoughs. I can taste that stuff yet.

And how many things you learned as you went along! Sentimental young folks still take stock in that beautiful old saying that when the baby smiles in his sleep, it is because the angels are whispering to him. Very pretty, but too thin— simply wind on the stomach, my friends.

If the baby proposed to take a walk at his usual hour, two o'clock in the morning, didn't you rise up promptly and remark, with a mental addition which would not improve a

Sunday school book much, that that was the very thing you
were about to propose yourself?

Oh, you were under good discipline, and as you went
fluttering up and down the room in your undress uniform,
you not only prattled undignified baby-talk, but even tuned
up your martial voices and tried to sing!—"Rock-a-by baby
in the tree-top," for instance.

What a spectacle for an Army of the Tennessee! And
what an affliction for the neighbors, too; for it is not everybody
within a mile around that likes military music at three in
the morning.

And when you had been keeping this sort of thing up
two or three hours, and your little velvet-head intimated that
nothing suited him like exercise and noise, what did you
do? ("Go on!") You simply went on until you dropped in
the last ditch.

The idea that a baby doesn't amount to anything! Why,
one baby is just a house and a front yard full by itself. One
baby can furnish more business than you and your whole
Interior Department can attend to. He is enterprising, ir-
repressible, brimful of lawless activities. Do what you please,
you can't make him stay on the reservation.

Sufficient unto the day is one baby. As long as you are
in your right mind don't you ever pray for twins. Twins
amount to a permanent riot. And there ain't any real difference between triplets and an insurrection.

Yes, it was high time for a toastmaster to recognize the
importance of the babies. Think what is in store for the
present crop! Fifty years from now we shall all be dead, I
trust, and then this flag, if it still survive (and let us hope it
may), will be floating over a Republic numbering two hundred
million souls, according to the settled laws of our increase.
Our present schooner of State will have grown into a political
leviathan. The cradled babies of today will be on deck. Let
them be well trained, for we are going to leave a big contract
on their hands. Among the three or four million cradles
now rocking in the land are some which this nation would

preserve for ages as sacred things, if we could know which ones they are.

In one of these cradles the unconscious Farragut of the future is at this moment teething—think of it!—and putting in a word of dead-earnest, unarticulated, but perfectly justifiable profanity over it, too.

In another the future renowned astronomer is blinking at the shining Milky Way with but a languid interest—poor little chap!—and wondering what has become of that other one they call the wet-nurse.

In another the future great historian is lying—and doubtless will continue to lie until his earthly mission is ended.

In another the future President is busying himself with no profounder problem of state than what the mischief has become of his hair so early; and in a mighty array of other cradles there are now some sixty thousand future office-seekers, getting ready to furnish him occasion to grapple with that same old problem a second time.

And in still one more cradle, somewhere under the flag, the future illustrious commander-in-chief of the American armies is so little burdened with his approaching grandeurs and responsibilities as to be giving his whole strategic mind at this moment to trying to find out some way to get his big toe in his mouth—an achievement which, meaning no disrespect, the illustrious guest of this evening turned his entire attention to some fifty-six years ago.

And if the child is but a prophecy of the man, there are mighty few who will doubt that he succeeded.

Humor and Emotion

Combining humor and emotion can be wonderfully effective. Leo Buscaglia, of television fame, is one of the most moving speakers in our society. As those who have enjoyed his lectures know, he conveys a great deal of warmth, which is precisely the proper tone, given that he lectures chiefly about the emotions. But, again, Buscaglia's openhearted, loving manner would not be appropriate to a speech about a scientific matter, sports, chess, or a corporation's quarterly report.

Nevertheless, I recommend the exercise of simply watching Buscaglia on television—or in person, for that matter. Notice how freely he speaks, how natural his gestures are, how easily he communicates with his listeners, how effectively he moves them, and—in the end—how well he instructs them.

When watching the experts—and this applies to any field, not just public speaking—it is not that you are under the obligation to become as gifted as they are, but simply that such good examples point you in the right direction. It would be a mistake to solemnly swear to yourself that you are going to become just as good at your task as Oscar Peterson, Sugar Ray Leonard, Martina Navratilova, Jimmy Connors, or Al Pacino, because the almost certain failure to achieve such rare levels of excellence could make you think that you had failed when, in fact, you had made remarkable progress.

Chapter 8

Speaking in Unusual Circumstances

As I have observed earlier, simple mastery of the knack of delivering a good speech does not quite cover the entire territory. The speaker must be prepared for surprises, variations on themes, and unusual circumstances of various sorts. In this chapter we'll touch on a few examples. You won't run into all of them early in your career as a public speaker, but in time you probably will, so it's never too early to begin giving them some thought.

Audience-Related Situations

A Small Audience in a Large Room

All the great actors of history have upon occasion performed to a small audience. They may be appearing in a poor-quality play. Perhaps a rainstorm or extreme cold spell is responsible. Perhaps advance promotion and publicity have been inadequate. So if it happens to the greats, don't take it too personally if it happens to you. Admittedly, looking out into an auditorium that seats five hundred and seeing about seventy-five people waiting to hear you isn't the most pleasant experience in the world, but you can actually make use of it to get sympathy for your predicament and even as raw material for a humorous approach. "Good evening, ladies and gentlemen—and seats" is a line that some comedians have used to good effect in such instances.

Another old line you might employ—if you think you can carry off such banter—is "You think *this* is bad? I gave a speech in Cleveland last week with an audience this size, and three empty seats got up and walked out."

Here's a mini-routine I once ad-libbed and have since occasionally repeated, when confronted with the same situation.

One of the fascinating things about entertaining and lecturing is that I get to address so many different kinds of audiences. I appeared on a comedy special on CBS last Tuesday, and the network told me that thirty-five million people saw that program. Three nights later I filled in for Johnny Carson on the *Tonight* show, and I understand there were about ten million viewers watching that evening. And now—look at this.

But don't worry, ladies and gentlemen, because what you lack in quantity—you also would appear to lack in quality, as I now get a better look at you.

On another occasion, at a dinner attended by fewer than had been anticipated, I said, "I don't feel bad about the size of this audience, ladies and gentlemen, so there's no reason you should, either. Jesus Christ addressed a very small gathering at the Last Supper. And he didn't get many laughs, either, come to think of it."

But even short of such one-liners you can, simply by adopting a good-natured tone, derive some personal benefit from the situation. If a good part of your audience is seated in the back of the room, as is often the case in such predicaments, encourage them to move forward so that they constitute a close, intimate crowd after all, even if small in number.

An Unsympathetic Audience

At this early stage of your development as an orator I wouldn't worry too much about the possibility of encountering a hostile audience. However, if you persist in your efforts—in fact, if you turn out to be rather good at public speaking—and if, secondly, one or another of your addresses advocates a clear-cut position on some important issue, it's likely that you will eventually confront unfriendly individuals in an average audience, or a largely hostile crowd itself.

Be of good cheer. Nobody is actually going to come up and hit you, or throw things. Well, wait a minute. There was that one time when eggs and tomatoes were thrown, but once isn't too bad considering that I've been speaking in public for some forty years. On the occasion in question I was in a large hall in Boston, Massachusetts, speaking about the dangers of nuclear radiation and atomic war. A number of prominent Americans were on the platform, addressing an audience of perhaps ten thousand, the great majority of whom were friendly, or at least neutral. But there were three or four hooligans from a right-wing extremist organization, and at one point they demonstrated the degree of their civilization by throwing eggs, one of which splattered a distinguished American scholar. The primary reaction, fortunately, was a wave of sympathy for those on the platform and vigorous booing directed at the culprits, who in any event ran out of the hall chased by police.

In an audience of that size you rarely see individual faces, so the psychological dynamics of the situation are quite different from what you experience when addressing two or three hundred. I ran into a few largely hostile audiences of the more intimate sort some years ago, having responded to invitations from conservative groups to address them. On one occasion the experience was so bizarre that I found it utterly fascinating and instructive.

A gentlemanly young fellow, a member of Young Americans for Freedom, a conservative organization, had sent me a cordial letter inviting me to explain to an audience of his philosophical allies the reasons why I thought our society faced a danger from atmospheric nuclear testing, not to mention the daily stockpiling of weapons of mass destruction.

I accepted his invitation and showed up at a small meeting hall in the Los Angeles area. The young gentleman and a couple of his friends greeted me warmly and took me into the room. It soon became apparent that their humane attitude was not shared by all present. As I sat waiting to be introduced I studied the faces of some of the people in the first few rows. Most were blank enough, some bore the faint polite smiles of welcome that one might encounter in addressing any audience, and three or four struck me as comic because of the spiteful, almost maniacal glares being directed toward me.

I delivered my talk without further dramatic incident, but the question-and-answer period was something else. One middle-aged man in the front row—he looked, physically, like the sort of actor who is usually cast as a Nazi SS guard in movies about World War II—literally could not contain himself when he rose to ask a question. Instead of simply standing, he lunged—ran, actually—seven or eight steps toward me, stopping just short of the low platform on which I stood. His face was red, his voice choked with emotion, his fist clenched, as he asked God knows what inane question; I can't recall what it was after so many years. There was no difficulty answering it, in any event, and the rest of the evening flowed smoothly enough past that awkward moment.

A few minutes later, as I was leaving, the young fellows who had invited me walked me to my car.

"I'm terribly sorry," one of them said. "There are always a few nuts in the audience. You know how it is."

"Certainly," I said. "Don't give the matter another thought. I appreciate your invitation because I get a little tired of talking to people who already agree with me. It's more interesting to address those with other points of view."

But again, the purpose of telling you the story is to let you know that one does survive even such experiences.

Needless to say, there are nuts and kooks (to use Richard Nixon's term) on the political far left, too. If you're a conservative you might one day find yourself heckled by some of them. Keep in mind that a sense of humor about the situation can be invaluable, as William F. Buckley often demonstrates. His sort of genial charm, although it is unfortunately sometimes tinged with arrogance, is nevertheless far preferable to a cranky approach to antagonistic audiences.

Your actual remarks to unfriendly audiences, however, should never be the standard word-for-word talk that you might have given previously on the same subject. You must *incorporate* the knowledge that there are those present who differ with you on the issue at hand, and modify the development of your argument accordingly. You might, for example, say something like "Now, I know a number of you here this evening differ with me on this particular point, but I very much appreciate your having invited me to speak to you about the matter, because it gives me the opportunity to explain why I feel as I do."

If you say something of that sort, in a cordial tone, the majority of your audience will show you the courtesy of at least listening. Don't expect that everyone present will be converted to your position on the spot, but at least you have the opportunity to engage in reasonable dialogue, one of the distinguishing marks of a civilized society.

I reemphasize the importance of keeping the bias of your hearers in mind, because it is essential. Is your audience largely Christian? Mormon? Catholic? Jewish? Communist? Anticommunist? Republican? Democrat? Such factors must affect the content of your remarks.

I once addressed an audience in which there were a number of Catholics, and I could see the effect on them of a point based on the Catholic belief in a literal hell in which sinners will actually burn—in the flesh—for all eternity. I explained that there were hundreds of millions of people on earth who believed in the literalness of hell just as firmly as they believed that George Washington was the first President of the United States. Then I reminded them that those who are thought to go to hell are simply any who die having committed serious sins but without having repented for them and obtained God's forgiveness.

I said to them, "Now, consider exactly what a nuclear war would involve. It would all be over in a few hours and would, of course, involve surprise attack. Scores of millions of people—in many parts of the world—would simply be incinerated instantly, as were thousands at Hiroshima and Nagasaki. There would be no time for repentance. So if those Christians are correct who believe in the literalness of hell, then we know that a nuclear war would greatly increase the population of hell."

I'm not suggesting that my argument would have awed Thomas Aquinas; merely that it was perfectly suited to the interests and biases of that particular audience.

An Audience That Knows More About the Subject Than You Do

This sort of thing—which, in a totally rational society would probably not occur at all—is nevertheless common in ours. Candidates for public office, and public figures of other kinds as well, frequently find themselves addressing people who are better informed on the subject at hand than the speaker. You might, for example, deliver a lecture on education to an audience consisting largely of teachers. You might speak on athletics to a group of athletes, athletic directors, or coaches. You might give a talk on the prison system to an audience consisting of convicts, prison personnel, or parole officers.

First of all, don't worry unduly. There must be some reason you were asked to address such an audience.

I once lectured on mental health to a convention audience consisting entirely of psychiatrists and their spouses. I knew that I could not simply launch into the subject matter, even though my remarks were researched and sound enough that they were later published in a psychiatric journal. The situation seemed to call for some sort of qualification, an explanation as to why such an invitation had been extended and why I had accepted it. After a few minutes of considering the problem I thought of a solution. A lifelong radio announcer and film actor, Ronald Reagan, who had never had any political experience whatever, had just been elected governor of California. I therefore said, "It may occur to some of you to wonder what can be the profit in listening to a speech by someone who knows a great deal less about the subject than you do. That originally gave me pause. Then I recalled that this meeting takes place in the state of California, where it has recently been established that it is by no means necessary to know as much as those to whom one lectures." Because the remark was greeted with hearty laughter and applause, the audience was put into a suitable frame of mind to receive the rest of the speech, which was of an entirely serious nature.

If you want to adapt the line to your own purposes, you might say, "I'm well aware that many of you in the audience are better informed on the subject than I am, but after all I'm only availing myself of the same opportunity that we accord to politicians every day of the week. They, too, sometimes lecture to us about things we know more about than they do." You might also quote Will Rogers' line, "We're all ignorant, only on different subjects," and then suggest that there are perhaps certain aspects of the large question concerning which the audience might find your views of interest, despite their own general sophistication.

An Infant Crying in the Audience

In most cases the parent will have the good sense to solve the problem by pacifying the child so that the crying stops, or by quietly taking the child out of the room. Once in a great while, however, the problem persists. The late Bishop Fulton J. Sheen was once interrupted by the wail of a small child while delivering one of his superb sermons. After a moment the mother picked up the baby and began to tiptoe out.

"The child isn't bothering me," Bishop Sheen said.

"I know," replied the mother, "but you're bothering her."

You're unlikely to conclude the drama with that sort of laugh, so you must be prepared for the possibility of interrupting your talk and addressing the situation directly. You should, of course, be kind in so doing, but there may come a point when the interruption may no longer be safely ignored.

In such a predicament I once said, "As the father of four sons I've more than once been in the position of the parents of that child. Personally I could go on even if there were several children crying at the same time, but I know that most people are too distracted by that sort of thing to concentrate on what is being said. So if you wouldn't mind taking the child out—at least until he stops crying—

I'm sure the rest of our audience would appreciate it." The response was applause and gracious cooperation from the parents.

Audience Participation

After you've acquired some experience and developed confidence as a speaker, you might care to add elements of audience participation to your repertoire. You've probably been present at certain outdoor coliseums where speakers have asked everyone present to light a match. The sudden spectacle of fifty or one hundred thousand small flames glowing in the darkness is quite impressive. It is frequently used to make a point such as "Ladies and gentlemen, this demonstrates what we can do if we all act in unison" or "By this simple act we have shown a modern application of Shakespeare's observation about how far the candle throws its beam."

Edward Hegarty, whose *Humor and Eloquence in Public Speaking* (Parker) I recommend to you, tells of a speaker he once saw who employed audience participation in a dramatically effective way.

> He was talking to a luncheon club about contributing to relief of an area that had been hit by a tornado. The news report said that seventy percent of the people had been killed or disabled. The room was set up ten people at each round table. He asked three persons at each table to stand. Then he said, "I tell you *seventy percent* and you can't picture it. But here you can see it. You people sitting are dead or disabled. You three standing have to take care of the mess. You'd need help, wouldn't you?"

I once ad-libbed a line that worked so effectively that I've used it occasionally since, in certain situations. After being introduced to an audience in a radio studio I said, "By the way, how many of you folks have never been here before?" At that I held my hand aloft to demonstrate that I wanted new visitors to do the same. About three-quarters of the audience held hands high. I then said, "All right. Now—how many of you are here tonight for the first *time?*" About half of those present started to lift their hands again and then broke into hearty laughter.

Today's young comedians often employ similar devices to begin their acts. They might ask, "How many of you are into astrology?" "How many of you are trying to give up smoking?" "Anybody here born in a small town?" or something of the sort. Such questions immediately get the audience personally involved, which can be helpful to both speakers and entertainers.

Speaking When You're Introduced but Unprepared

For most speakers this can be the most unnerving experience of all. Even though I've been speaking and entertaining for some four decades, I'm occasionally thrown off balance when someone says, "Incidentally, folks, I know you'd all be disappointed if we didn't get Steve Allen up here to say a few words—." Naturally you cannot be so surprised if you're the main speaker, but it sometimes happens if there are a number of details to an evening's program and the master of ceremonies gets the bright idea that there ought to be one more speaker.

I once visited a number of California prisons with the late philosopher-author Gerald Heard. At Atascadero, which housed chiefly prisoners convicted of serious sexual crimes, I sat on the platform listening to a brief talk by Mr. Heard, after which I was suddenly numbed to hear the warden say, "And now I'm sure we'd all enjoy hearing from Steve Allen."

Here I was, totally unprepared, and facing a somewhat sullen crowd of hardened sex offenders. During the few seconds it took to approach the microphone I was unable to think of any resolution at all to the predicament of the moment. A few seconds later I heard myself say, "Gentlemen, I address you today as one who hasn't been caught yet."

The line got a rousing reception, after which I delivered myself of a few observations on the subject of crime and punishment, concerning which I had fortunately done considerable study.

If you ever find yourself in a similar situation, you might take some sort of encouragement from my "solution" to it, or from the equally peculiar solution spontaneously devised by the late Allan Sherman, who in 1941 took a course in speaking at the University of Illinois. Although he had been assigned to deliver a five-minute speech, he did not go to the trouble of preparing even so much as a single sentence, much less a whole speech. With his mind a total blank he walked to the lectern, hemmed and hawed, then cleared his throat and said, "I shall give an illustrated lecture on the interior of the human mouth, the teeth, the tongue, the upper palate, the lower palate, and other points of interest," after which he proceeded to do exactly that.

It's important to recall here that although unexpected introductions make me ill at ease, I nevertheless have never once failed to deliver the goods in such a situation. At such moments, you depend first of all on the simple factor of human speech that has enabled you to communicate with individuals all your life. As I mentioned earlier, you are not handed a script for the day every morning when you get out of bed.

What can you do in such situations? The first thing to do is to be prepared for them. I don't mean to have some sort of stock five-minute ad-lib address tucked in the back of your head for such occasions. Even if you prepared for such a talk you'd probably forget it between the time it was constructed and the time someone actually called you up by surprise. But you can, nevertheless, have a collection of just four or five points that it might be reasonable to make in such a situation. You might, for example, have a joke or two that you've heard someone tell or that you've previously used yourself.

Second, you might have prepared some observation about how annoying it is to have someone call upon you to make a few remarks when your mind is absolutely blank. You might say something like "And if you've heard the *earlier* speakers this evening you'll *know* why my mind is blank."

Third, you might profitably forget *yourself* totally. Simply refer to the business of the evening. There was presumably some worthwhile social purpose which drew all hands together—a Red Cross drive, a church social, a political rally, a meeting to support some worthy cause—so you may briefly refer to that unifying theme.

Don't feel, by the way, that you have to prepare such "extemporaneous" remarks only because you're an amateur. Most professionals do it, so you're in good company.

Of course, you're ahead of the game if you've got a sense of humor, because it's quite possible that during the evening something will have occurred to which you can now refer. Did you notice anything peculiar about the audio system in the room? About the lighting? About one of the previous speakers? Was the sound of a siren heard in the street outside the hall? Was there anything at all that the audience might have noticed that could now provide a basis for some comment?

If, despite my advice and your own best intentions, a situation arises in which you are called upon with no advance warning and you find yourself completely blank, you might consider saying something along the following lines:

Like the rest of you, I've enjoyed this evening's program. Mr. Jones gave an entertaining talk, and I know that we're all united in the purpose for which this meeting was convened. Since I've been a member of this audience for the past two hours, I'm well aware that it's a superior audience, if I do say so myself. As a speaker it would be my great pleasure to address you formally on some future occasion. But the hour is late, we've already heard a number of other very fine comments, and I know most of you aren't looking forward to eagerly standing in line in the cold outside waiting for the parking attendants to bring your cars up out of the garage, so I'll just say in closing that—

As you'll see, there's no requirement whatever to deliver oratory that would put Lincoln's Gettysburg Address or William Jennings Bryan's Cross of Gold speech to shame. The audience will be quite content with just a few sincere or possibly light and amusing comments. If you have become a famous speaker, they will be grateful for even a few minutes of your time. And if you're not illustrious, they'll be just as relieved that you don't ramble on.

Speaking in a Large Stadium

Addressing a crowd of seventy-five or a hundred thousand at some athletic stadium may be something you'll never experience. Nevertheless, since it's possible, you ought to be prepared for the fact that in most such locations you will have to speak in short sentences. I discovered this the hard way by saying a few words at Yankee Stadium in New York.

I launched at once into my usual chatter but was brought up short before I had completed the first sentence. After so many years I have no recollection of what I said, but let's assume it was something like "Good evening, ladies and gentlemen, I'm very honored to be part of this important program tonight." Well, I got about as far as "Good evening, ladies and gentlemen, I'm very—" At that point, just as I was prepared to continue with the rest of the thought, I suddenly heard the first few words of the sentence floating back to me. This not only surprised me but knocked the rest of the sentence completely out of my mind. I made the necessary adjustments at once, but it was still an unnerving experience to have to speak in staccato bursts and then wait, in silence, for the words to come back to me.

A slight variation on this mechanical problem is that in some large auditoriums you may occasionally run into an echo, so that what both you and the audience hear sounds something like this: "Good evening, evening, evening, ladies and gentlemen, gentlemen, gentlemen." That's a little hard to deal with, too, but at least it has the fortunate effect of preventing any terribly long speeches.

Debating

The one sort of speech for which it is absolutely necessary to do the most thorough preparation possible is that which takes place in the context of a debate. It isn't that being officially or informally declared the winner of a debate is a matter of the most earthshaking importance; it's just that you will be expected to give as able a presentation of your case as possible. Those who already agree with you will probably think you're the winner; those who differ will probably think your opponent did the better job. But even those who might feel that you were outclassed can still learn a good deal by your argument. So even if you're the loser a great deal might have been gained.

However, even this rule about the necessity for careful preparation is not absolutely ironclad. You may, for example, be so remarkably knowledgeable about the subject matter that you don't have to do any homework at all. But unless you *are* so eminently qualified, you will be well advised to devote time to the construction of your case.

Unless you are yourself a recognized authority on the subject at hand, you ought to refer to others who are. And in this context recall my earlier recommendations that you keep the general social makeup of your audience in mind. If, for example, all or a good many of those present are Catholics, it wouldn't be the wisest thing in the world to quote Karl Marx, Mary Baker Eddy, Bertrand Russell, Madalyn Murray O'Hair, or Martin Luther. But a quotation from the New Testament or from Saint Thomas Aquinas, Saint Augustine, a Pope, or the late Bishop Sheen would have considerable impact.

It is also helpful if you not only understand your own position fully but make an attempt to grasp the other fellow's side of the case, particularly beforehand. Failure to attend to that detail can leave you hanging on the ropes if your opponent suddenly introduces a line of speculation, an argument, or a fact that had simply never occurred to you.

Another tip: Forget yourself totally once the debate starts, particularly while your opponent is speaking. Listen intently to everything he says and make notes of any points on which you think he is vulnerable.

Parliamentary Procedure

A good part of public speaking in the American context takes place at formal meetings. You might be a member of an organization—a service, a club, a school board, a church group, or a union—that holds meetings at which either officials or visitors are permitted to speak. If you are called upon to participate in such a context, you must then take the trouble to familiarize yourself with parliamentary procedure.

Your neighborhood library or bookstore can provide textual material. Perhaps the best known compendium of such formalities is *Robert's Rules of Order*, originally published in 1876. Study it, naturally, but don't imagine that just half an hour of such reading will make you a fully qualified parliamentarian. Attend a few meetings. See how the game is played. You'll notice at once why it was necessary to establish firm rules.

Payment for Your Services?

Although the thought may never have occurred to you, the fact is that you can earn quite a good living by public speaking, at least if you are reasonably competent. Most speakers are not paid, of course, since they have their own reasons for being willing to address audiences. Lecturing for a fee is now, however, an important business enterprise. The number of gifted speakers is so limited that those who have the knack could, if they wished, occupy their time seven nights a week speaking at one public function or another.

True celebrities—show-business figures, famous authors, political leaders, eminent scholars—may be paid anywhere from $1000 to $15,000 for an evening's performance. Fees for most speakers, of course, are far more modest, sometimes running to just $50 to $100. A modest fee is referred to as an honorarium. It would be difficult to support a family on honoraria unless you worked at it full-time.

If you're new at the game, you need not give this aspect any further consideration for quite a long while. In time, though, the word does get around about those speakers who are especially polished. This does not mean that any audience at all will pay to hear you lecture on any subject. Particular audiences want to hear particular sorts of messages. Audiences are shoppers, too.

Chapter 9

Accepting an Award or Other Honor

Sometimes people who have avoided making speeches for their entire lives are nevertheless finally trapped simply because they have been presented with an honorary degree or some other award for meritorious service to society.

What sort of speech should you make in accepting the award? A *short* one.

A great deal depends, of course, on who you are. If you're Henry Kissinger, Gore Vidal, Norman Cousins, or a former President of the United States, the audience will be pleased to hear you carry on for a while. But if you're some average citizen who has worked very hard for one particular worthy cause or another, restrain yourself. The presenter of the award has already talked enough about you; you don't have to continue at any length on that subject.

Because my good friend Pat Harrington, Jr.—a regular member of our old television comedy gang and more recently one of the stars of the popular television series *One Day at a Time*—is funny, he struck just the proper note, I think, in responding to an award presented to him in 1980 by the Christian Brothers. I would have been happy to publish my own response here, since the Christian Brothers were kind enough to bestow their annual citation on Jayne and me a few years ago, but that particular address seems to have slipped through a crack, so I'm including Pat's as an excellent example of the genre.

Pat is, of course, a professional comedian. If you're a distinguished ophthalmologist, economist, or philosopher, something less facetious would be indicated. The important thing is to be yourself and respond in what is a reasonable way for you.

Thank you, Brother Dominic, for that lovely introduction. I've seldom heard one more impressive or accurate.

And may I say, "Good evening to you, the St. John the Baptiste de la Salle, La Sallian Ambassadors of the Western Province of the Fellowship of Christian Brothers of the World . . . Inc." That is, without question, the most ridiculous title any organization, anywhere, has ever called itself.

I mean I could go along with the "The Western Province Winos," or something. For one thing, you'd never get that other name on your bowling shirt.

Now, on the other hand, my full name is concise and to the point, Pat "Actor" Harrington. That may strike you as an unusual middle name. Actually, I got the idea many years ago from Francis Cardinal Spellman.

The Cardinal and I are both New Yorkers, only I was born in Hell's Kitchen on Manhattan's West Side. That made me a lower-middle-class Irish-Catholic Democrat. Today, I live in Bel Air, California. An upper-middle-class Roman Catholic Republican.

In point of fact, I've changed very little. The only difference is today, I can hire people to say my penance.

It might be useful if you know that my education consists of the following:

8 years . . . Sisters of Mary and Joseph at St. Paul the Apostle School, New York;

4 years . . . Christian Brothers at La Salle Military Academy, Oakdale, Long Island;

4 years with the Jesuits at Fordham University, Bronx, New York.

That's 16 years of Catholic education. 16 years. That's about what you get nowadays for grand theft auto.

I think it's appropriate at this time to say that I am, indeed, flattered to be chosen this year as the recipient of your annual award. On the other hand, don't let it go to your head. You're not looking at some yo-yo who's never received anything. I mean, in the last month alone, I have received the Rona Barret Award for the best male actor on *One Day at a Time.*

And on the very day I was asked to receive your prestigious award, I also received an invitation to attend the Annual Blessing of the Grapes from Ernie and Julio Gallo. As you know, from time to time Julio likes to dress up as a bishop. César Chávez went in my stead.

Actually, accepting the La Sallian Ambassador's award was not a difficult decision at all. Your award is truly unique. As I am sure you are aware, it is given each year to an individual who has basically met three requirements:

1. Achieved great success in his chosen field. (In my case 5 straight years of employment with three beautiful women . . . enough said.)

2. Performed great service to the community. (Some would argue that lowering property values in Bel Air is indeed a great community service.)
    and

3. Represents the highest ideals in his personal life . . .

How did you find that out?
I was under the impression that only my wife and kids

knew of the high ideals of my personal life. Well, maybe a couple of neighbors who may have heard Marge and me talking about my high ideals. Okay, yelling about them.

I think I know how you found out. Every Sunday morning, for as long as I can remember, a couple of well-dressed young people have been knocking on my front door . . . trying to sell me a subscription to something called *The Watchtower* . . . and they always questioned me about my ideals and things. I thought they were members of Jehovah's Allies or something. But I think now it was really a couple of undercover agents for the La Sallian Ambassadors, poking around trying to find out all about my high ideals. I should report you people to the archdiocese.

But the archdiocese doesn't talk to people who go to confession to Father Keiser. I've known Elwood Keiser for twenty years. Do you know what it's like going to confession to a man whose show occasionally outranks your own? Last week he gave me thirteen Hail Mary's with an option for six more.

In any case, the important thing is that the La Sallian award concerns itself with success, service, and personal values. Let me suggest that in my case you should have included a fourth ingredient: luck . . . great gobs of luck! Much more than was recently needed, for example, by the U.S. Olympic hockey team.

And if you don't agree that our hockey team was indeed lucky, consider for a moment the astonishing fact that the high scoring first line on our team was composed of two guys named Harrington and Schneider.

But we're talking about luck, and the point is this: When I joined the Screen Actors Guild in 1955, its membership was 14,000. At that time there were available on any given day, perhaps a thousand acting or acting-related jobs. Today the guild membership is swollen to 47,000 and the job pool is approximately 750.

Notwithstanding the frightening implications of these figures, you're looking at a man who has been steadily employed, as I mentioned earlier, for five consecutive years. Statistically, this puts me in the top one-tenth of one percent of all actors anywhere in this country. Now, I know I'm talented, folks, but I'm not that talented. That requires a lot of luck—pure and simple. You and I both realize that a lot of American Oliviers are out there somewhere getting old and discouraged.

Now, then, add to this good fortune the incredible bonus of being associated with the Norman Lear organization, and believe me, ladies and gentlemen, that is an enormous bonus. With the help of Carroll O'Connor's classic Irish face and talent, Lear changed the structure of American television irrevocably. *All in the Family* made all previous situation comedies instantly irrelevant. It was the first program of its type that had anything new or different to say. And Lear followed this watershed contribution with a string of equally provocative successes: *Maude, Sanford and Son, The Jeffersons, Mary Hartman, Mary Hartman*, and finally, thank God, *One Day at a Time*.

Let me review for you just some of the subjects our little sitcom has concerned itself with over the past five years. I'll mention the show title first.

1. "Chicago Rendezvous": You're a divorcée and you're spending the weekend with a lover. Do you or don't you tell your young teenage daughters?

2. "J.C. and Julie": At what point does piety and sanctity become fanaticism? How does a parent attempt to reverse the process?

3. "All the Way": How does a single parent help her young daughter discern the responsibilities and consequences of premarital sex?

4. "Schneider's Helper": How the mentally retarded can be made aware of their own precious usefulness through compassion and understanding.

5. "Ann's Secretary": The inhumanity of contemporary

hiring practices relative to people with covert diseases. In this case, epilepsy.

6. "The Married Man": The complex mix of moral and social values which characterize an affair with a married partner.

7. "Peabody's War": The cultural and moral consequences of warehousing our senior citizens.

8. "Barbara's Friend": Teenage suicide.

9. "The Ghost-Writer": Academic dishonor.

10. "Schneider the Model": Male menopause.

As you can see, it's just been five years of one laugh after another. . . .

Obviously, what we have here, without the character of Schneider, is situation tragedy. I kind of see myself as playing George "Gabby" Hayes to Bonnie Franklin's Roy Rogers. Don't tell Bonnie.

Or maybe, don't tell Roy.

But hand in hand with such popularity and prestige is the individual's responsibility to participate as fully as he can in the collaborative effort required to produce such a program. And let me assure you, right here, that one's religious education can have a marked effect on the quality and intensity of that participation.

Long before my association with *One Day at a Time* I remember huddling with the Dean of Philosophy at Loyola Marymount University about whether or not I should undertake the lead in a local production of a new play by the German author Rolf Hochhuth. Perhaps some of you recall his play *The Deputy*, a forceful indictment of Pope Pius XII's handling of the Jewish question during World War Two. I think we finally decided that I might do the role only if I were sure it was a genuine artistic endeavor, and not, in fact, a religious polemic seeking to spread blame. I couldn't resolve that question, so I didn't do it.

The point is that because of my background, my tutelage

by the Sister Theresas, the Brother Johns, and the Father McGanns of the American Catholic educational establishment, I've been sensitized to perceive, and I feel equipped to address that kind of problem. I also feel eminently qualified to jump feetfirst into something as raucous as the weekly creative slugfest down at *One Day at a Time*.

It's quite beautiful, really. Every Monday morning at 11 o'clock, twenty or so people sit around a large table in rehearsal hall F at Metromedia Square in Hollywood and proceed to disagree for the next five days.

We have Mormons, Jews, Baptists, atheists . . . you name it, we have it . . . and, of course, we have one mustachioed little Irishman, educated and prepared by, amongst others, the Christian Brothers. In the past five years I haven't hesitated one bit from making myself one enormous royal pain in the elbow. Whether it concerned character, theme, structure or an insignificant little straight line for a joke, I gave my opinion on why it was wrong and how it should be done.

Sometimes I was even right.

For example, Schneider started out as an adulterer. I changed that. He began as a shallow, manipulative neurotic. I changed that. He was a boastful, vain male chauvinist. . . . That I kept . . . well, that's funny.

I'm not sure, but I honestly think the show is somewhat better because of this kind of caring and participation. And, of course, in some small, imperceptible way, the message of the Christian Brothers is being echoed, from time to time, on Sunday nights at 8:30.

A moment ago I mentioned some of the themes our show has dealt with and some of the awards we've received. I am very proud of the fact that three of those stories—"Ann's Secretary," "Schneider the Model" and "Peabody's War"—were written by my partner and myself. I might also mention that two of those three shows received national awards . . . but who's keeping score?

I am what I am and I guess I'll never change my stripes . . .

and really that's not all bad. A friend who graduated from Fordham with me moved to a small town in the South. Shortly after he got there the KKK found out he was Catholic and they burned a cross on his lawn. Overcome with fear and anxiety, he left the church and became a Unitarian. He thought the KKK wouldn't know what that was. And he was right. The following week they burned a question mark on his lawn. So what did he gain?

I want to thank you very much for honoring me this evening. Frankly, I think you're much too generous with your award. Steve Allen should never have gotten it.

But Steve and I are both familiar with the old show-biz axiom: "Take the award and run," so that's exactly what I am going to do.

I hope you all have a pleasant, fun-filled Lent. I've been watching you since you arrived, and it's nice to see that you haven't given up anything important except this award.

Thank you.

An excellent address—witty, informative, and thoughtful.

I should remind you that the purpose of including speeches here—others' or my own—is to solicit your active, not passive, response. You are, obviously, free to think about one quoted speech or another, "My, isn't that impressive?" or "I don't think this is very good at all." But whether you approve or disapprove—or a combination of both—you should ask *why* your opinion was formed. Break the speeches down into their constituent parts, analyze, be critical. Note how the separate thoughts are joined together.

Does the speaker capture your attention in the first sentence or paragraph? If not, why not? If so, how so?

One of the most delightful short speeches was made by actress Katharine Hepburn in accepting a Screen Actors Guild award on January 27, 1980. Ms. Hepburn made a tape recording of her remarks, and they were played to a Guild Award dinner. Whil comments are typically Hepburn—which is to say cha sightful, and heartwarming—an analysis of her speech will never-theless profit the reader, for it shows the importance of sincerity and an open expression of such emotion as the speaker might feel.

Good afternoon, everybody—I should say, fellow work-ers. That makes it sound revolutionary. This is the letter that I wrote Bill Schallert when he wrote me that you had chosen me: "I am dumbfounded, and at the same time, I am very proud to have been chosen by the Screen Actors Guild as a good example, professionally and personally. It is always heartening to be told by one's fellows that one is first rate, and that they wish to say so publicly.

"Sitting here in my New York house, I enjoyed this news immensely. But if I had to go to California and accept this award, it would really make me a very miserable creature, as this sort of appearance is torture to me. I hope that they will understand how very, very happy I am they have made me their choice, and allow me the sweet privilege of enjoying it in private.

"With great many thanks to them and you for this great honor."

Now that's what I wrote to Bill Schallert. And now I am going to try to say to you what I feel secretly.

All the funny, the curious thoughts which assail one when a group of people, your own group, give you a pat on the back. And I thought of my family, my private family—I've been very lucky. I am one of six. I still live where I grew up. I am still friends with the man with whom I won the three-legged race in 1917. I have had community and I have had safety. Now I suddenly realize that I have a professional family. You. All my fellows. We all do the same things, more or less.

We have similar ambitions. We are traveling along the same road, so to speak. And I think: I am your sister. Well, I'm your mother, or I might be your grandmother more aptly. And you are mine and I am yours. And I am safe. Well, not safe. No one is safe. But I am protected by this union if I am sick or hopeless. And now you all get together and you give me the prize. That's very heartwarming.

And I think to myself, "You're too big a pig to go out there and accept it. You're just an old pig." And then I think to myself, "Yes, you are. But you're *their* old pig and they love you, and they gave you a prize, and they proved it." So I sit back. I'm touched and I'm very moved. You've done a lot for me. Thank you.

Applause, applause, Miss Hepburn.

Chapter 10

Summing Up the Evening's Program

If you are the last speaker on a given occasion, you may be expected to not only deliver your own observations but also summarize, or at least comment upon, the remarks of earlier speakers.

I delivered the following speech to the Santa Barbara Social Psychiatry Workshop in March of 1971. It is a useful example to study in that it incorporates most of the component parts I have discussed in earlier chapters. Note that although the occasion was obviously a relatively serious one, a few touches of humor, handled properly, were not out of place. The speech was partly written, partly ad-libbed, and partly based on handwritten notes made during the proceedings described.

Summary of Workshop Proceedings

Thank you, Dr. Auerback, for your generous introduction. Since you raised the question as to whether—my parents being vaudevillians—I ever slept in a dresser drawer, the answer is no—we couldn't afford a dresser.

Well, this has been a most stimulating conference. I arrived here three days ago refreshed and energetic, eager for what was to come. Now, after three days of listening, speaking, taking notes, studying, and discussing from early morning till late at night, I am utterly exhausted. In which condition I am called upon to summarize these proceedings.

I am comforted, however, by the knowledge that the very futility of my assignment will merit your sympathy. In this connection I am reminded of a very funny story. But I shall resist the temptation to tell it.

The title of my address, like that of Mr. Rozenfeld's, as rendered in the program is inaccurate. It has no title. In a sense it isn't even an address. It's more an exercise in presumption.

Being an expert on nothing that has been discussed here, I am, of course, the most qualified to discuss everything, because I am uninhibited by those sharply defined professional boundaries that limit the rest of you.

I might be considered, in this context, a lay expert. No, come to think of it, I'm not even an expert on that. I throw in a bit of vulgarity here so that you young people will feel at home.

But, in all conceit, I have a few observations, and questions, about some of the things we have heard during these three stimulating days.

Since the discussions themselves did not follow—indeed, could not have followed—a straight, disciplined line of inquiry, my comments on them then constitute chiefly a catalogue of your modest digressions, to which I may perhaps add one or two of my own.

There were countless endearing indications, during these meetings, of our naive humanity, which it is always particularly refreshing to encounter in an assemblage of sophisticated practitioners of one professional discipline or another.

For example, even here, despite the fame and importance of a given speaker, despite the breadth of experience of members of this audience—and despite the great unlikelihood that the next person to walk into this room at a given moment might have been President Nixon, Mao Tse-tung, or the returned Christ—nevertheless, every time someone walked in during an address almost every head turned away from the speaker and glanced, however casually, toward the door.

And despite your depth of understanding and compassion, there were hostile glares directed at those seized by uncontrollable fits of coughing, and even at the inanimate device that is recording these proceedings.

The high-pitched, wavering tone it has emitted this morning I found first annoying, then nostalgically comforting in that it reminded me of the sound of the old radiators that heated so many of the rooms in which I lived as a child.

Dr. Auerback, intending to refer to Sarah Lawrence College, called it "David" Lawrence, and then, in response to your laughter, said, "Make of it what you will."

I respectfully suggest, Doctor, that in this professional context what is made of it will have to be what *you* will.

Dr. Erika Freeman has told us, among other interesting things, that in a sense England was our mother, France our mistress, and Germany our teacher.

She did not identify our *father*, which would seem to confirm our present low opinion of ourselves.

Her point that we ought to judge ideas on their merits rather than solely in regard to their source is precisely that which led to the development of a new game (for which I served as consultant) called *Strange Bedfellows*, one of a series designed to teach all of us how to think.

Dr. Tietz's reference to asterisks and the numerous and lengthy footnotes in his paper reminded me of an insight (or at least a crazy idea) that occurred to me some years ago when I participated in the experimental program on the effects of LSD conducted by Dr. Sydney Cohen at UCLA.

That was at a time, of course, before the abuse of the drug had emerged as a serious social problem.

I envisioned a page of a book, every word of which was followed by an asterisk, with footnotes.

But . . . in the footnotes, too, every word was followed by an asterisk.

In a time when many, particularly among the young, have grown increasingly cynical about the competence and dedication of political figures, it is encouraging to hear from so able and dedicated a public servant as Mr. Lanterman.

I was greatly enlightened by my exposure to Dr. Bierer's theories, impressed by his accomplishments, and charmed by his company.

Dr. Bierer believes that the solution to the mental health problems of our times is much too large and complex a job for psychiatrists and the mental health people alone. Dr. Auerback's sobering recital makes the dimensions of the problem alarmingly clear. The collaboration and involvement of a multidisciplinary group of professionals is clearly required. Even if Dr. Bierer were wrong philosophically, he is inescapably right on this point.

But his achievements argue persuasively for the essential validity of his approach, for he has contributed many significant innovations to social psychiatry: day and night hospitals, self-determining and self-governing therapeutic clubs, therapeutic communities, and others. Dr. Bierer believes that mental illness as such does not exist. He also believes— as now apparently every informed person does—that our system of legal justice and punishment is ineffective if not irrational.

One of the more interesting subsidiary questions raised concerns the extent to which the political Right, which has long been active in the field of mental health as the force of the opposition to it, is now making use of Dr. Szsaz and Dr. Bierer as weapons with which to attack psychiatry and the mental health movement generally. There are a number of historical factors involved in this rightist paranoia: (1) Anti-Semitism, because many psychiatrists are Jews, (2) the Churchversus-Freud, and (3) the suspiciousness characteristic of political fanaticism. Those who *need* treatment but deny the need are pleased to hear Dr. Bierer say, "There's no such thing as mental illness," because it confirms their sense of righteousness.

I am not referring to responsible conservatives here but to the traditional forces of know-nothing reaction.

The large question Dr. Bierer raises, being complex, is still unresolved. In recent years, as you know, there has been a return to emphasis, in some quarters, upon *physical* factors related to mental illness, if Dr. Bierer will pardon the expression.

That kind of genetic chromosomal abnormality, for example, which has a correlation with antisocial criminal behavior would be a case in point. There are studies, too, as you are aware, of differences in blood chemistry between those who are schizophrenics and those who are not. And there are the obvious questions presented by the successful results obtained by the administration of such drugs as *lithium* in modifying human behavior for the better.

It was only recently, historically speaking, that we discovered that separate parts of the brain governed separate bodily functions, muscular movements, speech, sight, memory, and so forth. But uncharted horizons now beckon in that specific area of the brain out of which the *emotions* arise.

I suspect little is known, too, about such refined areas of specialization as the *mathematical* or *musical* functions. If the strict environmentalists present will forgive me, it has always seemed to me preposterous to assert that if a genius can compose a symphony and play the piano brilliantly at the age of six, the fact is explained purely by the availability of a better-than-adequate music teacher.

I know from personal experience that the gift of musical composition has nothing whatever to do with being taught. The mechanical components of the art can be taught but the essential gift, the ability to synthesize factors in previously unimagined ways, is just that—if one posits a giver: a gift, a puzzling accident, difficult to explain even in terms of standard Darwinian theory, since it hardly is necessary to the survival of the species.

In a book written some years ago I advanced the hypothesis that the gift of religious spirituality, which is clearly more pronounced in some individuals than others, may have its focus literally in brain tissue. I hasten to add that since the firm belief that God made all things logically requires the belief that He created the human brain, the theory is in no way incompatible with religious philosophy generally.

It is interesting that some years later, when we began to receive reports, most of them scholarly and some of them from Dr. Bierer, attesting to either the reality or illusion of religious and spiritual insights under the influence of LSD and similar drugs, I began to feel that my theory was given substantial support in the form of consistent if by no means conclusive evidence.

Dr. Branch's presentation had the appeal we always sense in those arguments that conform with our own prejudices. I was especially intrigued by his reminding us of the importance of the emotional attitude of the therapist in relating to the patient, as dramatized in the story of the practitioner who reported that on five particular days his patients seemed especially cheerful and open. As you will recall, these were the days on which he had taken benzedrine.

This is consistent with my own experience in being frequently interviewed over a period of years, in connection with my television activities. I noticed early that the interviewers who were themselves extroverts tended to describe me as lively, witty, and genial, whereas those who were more introverted tended to describe me as shy, withdrawn, uncommunicative, etc.

There were a thousand and one tempting digressions, the following out of which could take literally many lifetimes. For example, Dr. Kennedy referred to *glossolalia*, the speaking in strange tongues.

I would like to know if tape recordings of the phenomenon have been made, if written transcripts of these recordings have been rendered, and if both have been subjected to analysis by disinterested linguistic scholars.

Dr. Kennedy's remarks struck a particularly responsive emotional chord.

One could not fail to be impressed by his enthusiasm for the campaign to, as he put it, *unscrew the pew.*

He expressed the idea with such force, in fact, that I would not be surprised to see him shortly dispense with the negative prefix.

But the relevance of the self-treating encounter group to the essential work of the church is clear. Just as Christians civilized the savage tribes of Europe, so the humanist tradition has worked tirelessly for centuries to civilize Christians. It is encouraging to observe that its influence continues unabated.

One of the most touching illustrations drawn by Dr. Kennedy concerned the man who was unable to weep at recollection of his own misfortunes but did so when one of the women in the group told him she loved him for his sympathetic response to her own recital.

The tears that flow in response to love are more mysterious than those that help relieve the sense of tragedy. I find that I am moved to tears at the spectacle of the reconciliation of enemies. There is a sudden rush of feeling that comes from the appreciation of the beautiful aspects of human communication.

I found Dr. Brill's presentation of particular interest, although perhaps at our next convocation we might be privileged to see a slide projection of that mysterious picture of him with the two Yugoslavian girls.

His description of the alienation of American youth was most complete and detailed. One must, it seems to me, agree with his conclusion that the state of consciousness of today's young people is different in kind, as well as in degree, compared to the youth of earlier generations.

One reason may be that today's technology—TV, radio, films, magazines, videotape, and audio equipment—brings our social reality into focus to a degree unprecedented in all history. And, in today's world, to become *aware* is to become *angry*.

One may become angry at the social injustice suffered by others or by oneself.

But it is remarkable how many ancient beliefs are currently relevant and popular among young people. As regards the materialistic biases of our generation, what are the young saying but that the love of money is the root of a great deal of evil?

In saying that they want to *enjoy* their work, not just perform it for money, the young are repeating the medieval theologians, are they not?

Unfortunately we resort to the specious as well as to what has been valid from the storehouse of history. Frank Kelly calls ours *The Age of Paranoia*. Who would have supposed it would follow the Age of Reason? And who would have predicted, in a period of spectacular scientific achievement, that the superstition of the Dark Ages, belief in witchcraft, astrology, fortune-telling, and diabolism would culminate in today's very similar wave of occultism and deliberate rejection of rational standards?

To the extent that the young regard the rest of us as enemies it might be argued that their position is most fortunate. For example, if you could tell the Marxists of the world that all capitalists will be dead in another 20 or 30 years, their joy would know no bounds. If you could assure the west that all communists would shortly vanish from our planet they, too, would be pleased. Well, the young can literally be assured that all of the older generation will be gone before long, after which the young will perceive that their most formidable adversaries are their own age.

And soon, all those who have said, "Don't listen to anybody over 30" will be over 30 themselves, and presumably without an audience.

As for the rebelliousness of today's youth, many of you must be tempted to hope that some magical method might be found whereby it could be stamped out. Not only is the hope utterly incapable of realization but, even if the thing were possible, it ought never to be done, for by inhibiting the rebellious instinct we would be running counter to one of mankind's most fundamental drives: the need to identify what is wrong in his physical context, to oppose what he regards as contemptible, and to construct a better social order. I naturally do not suggest that every fourteen-year-old who breaks a window consciously articulates such a philosophy, but rebellious acts as a class grow out of such a need and are consistent with such a philosophy. The rebel without a cause, as the brilliant Robert Lindner suggested, is dangerous. But the rebel with a good cause will be our salvation.

Both Dr. Brill and Dr. Girvetz commented on the problem of violence in today's youth culture. In my view, the underlying danger of violence, above and beyond the obvious physical destruction it causes—the deaths, the maimings, the personal tragedy—is that when it becomes institutionalized and apparently legitimized by philosophers or other spokesmen it unleashes dark, dangerous, poorly understood forces in the human heart, forces that may leap out and eventually consume those who called them forth.

In World War II we observed the atrocities committed by Germans and Japanese, while ignoring those perpetrated by ourselves and our allies. But the evildoers seemed more than evil in our eyes. All men, after all, are partly evil. Our enemy seemed monstrous. Clearly there were psychopaths, sadistic bullies, and other such wearing German uniforms. But I think most atrocities are committed by very average people, when they have been programmed to kill and absolved of guilt before the fact. The My Lai murders are a case in point.

I recall, in this connection, a young man who appeared

several years ago as a guest on one of my television programs. He had been captured by the Viet Cong while fighting in Vietnam and had been a prisoner for, as I recall, a year or so. Eventually he escaped and made his way back to safety.

When the program was over on the evening that he appeared, I invited him to join our production staff for our customary dinner in a restaurant near our theater in New York. I emphasize that this young man was very personable. He was, in a sense, the all-American boy. Not remarkably superior or inferior, he had a simple, rural, small-town-America manner about him. I would be very surprised to learn that he ever had suffered emotional problems of any sort. Nevertheless, while we were discussing the war with him, in answer to my question as to what he thought the ultimate solution might be, he said, "I think we ought to drop the bomb on the Chinese."

"You mean," I said, "attack China's military installations?"

"No," he said, "we ought just to wipe 'em all out."

"With hydrogen bombs?"

"Right."

"You mean," I said, "kill six or seven hundred million mostly civilian men, women, and children?"

"I know it sounds terrible," he said, "and it *would* be terrible. But, the way I look at it, we're going to have to fight them in the long run anyway. Better them than us."

So here we see an instance of a perfectly normal and I suppose essentially decent young fellow evidencing a moral insensitivity that is basically the sort that made the Nazis and more militant Japanese of World War II seem so monstrously evil from our point of view.

Dr. Girvetz's delineation of the problem of violence in our culture clearly suggested that it is on the increase, and side by side with the common view that today there is a greater incidence of mental and emotional disturbance in our society than at any time in our history, it is remarkable that Dr. Bierer's theories relating to doing away with mental hospitals and prisons are being advanced at a time when one might otherwise assume that they would be building *more* hospitals and prisons.

Another vitally important question, suggested by Mr. Kelly, is: In a presumably *representative* society, who really represents the people? It is not today the easiest question in the world to answer.

Part of the problem is that running for any political office is an incredibly expensive undertaking. Running for high office takes millions of dollars. The sources from which such funds are donated understandably enough expect some sort of return on their investment.

But in response to the growing awareness of this dilemma, there are signs of emerging programs designed to alleviate the distress. Ralph Nader and his organizations are a result of the feeling of helplessness on the part of the average citizen. *Common Cause* is another. So is the *consumer revolution* generally. Ombudsman experiments are springing up. Environmental conservationists are making their influence felt. Radio and TV stations are not only editorializing but are offering free time to spokesmen of points of view differing with those of station management.

I take these as hopeful indications.

At least two of our speakers, Mr. Rozenfeld and Dr. Cobbs, emphasized the destructive effects of inadequate social environments upon those forced to live in them. In the physical sense it has long been obvious that poverty and squalor lead to greater incidence of disease and a higher death rate. But only relatively recently have we learned of the harm that poverty does to the mind and the spirit.

Is it possible, however, that the harm is done in a secondary rather than direct sense, in that the conditions of the urban ghetto, as well as of rural poverty, tend to destroy the family, then bring the collapse of adequate parent-child relationships that directly cripples many children psychologically?

It is fascinating to observe to what extent the psychologically destructive potential of many of our unpleasant social problems is now being emphasized.

We have long known that litter, garbage, and sewerage are unedifying to observe, but we are now being told that they also contribute to our societal *neuroses.*

Perhaps one solution, in the context of our free-enterprise biases, would be to find a way to make sewerage and garbage commercially valuable. Then it would be responsibly handled.

Concerning racial confrontation, I found Dr. Cobbs' remarks of very great interest and I plan to read his book *Black Rage.*

In introducing him Dr. Brill observed that although over a million copies of his book had been sold, Dr. Cobbs reported receiving *very little money,* a fact which by itself would make his rage understandable.

One was pleased to hear his recommendation of the Jeffersonian approach to oppression. Almost everyone is opposed to some form of tyranny, but few seem to regard *all* forms as intolerable. Perhaps because most of our forefathers fled from oppression to these shores, Americans have long been opposed to all oppression except that which we perpetrated ourselves. But our foreign policy dilemma at present hangs on precisely the question as to how one should oppose oppression. Do we oppose it only within our national borders? If not, how do we respond to the pleas of the oppressed in other parts of the world? Neither of the two large alternatives is entirely satisfactory; consequently we grieve and are uncertain.

Small, revealing things hold a special sort of interest, whether we observe them in the behavior of individuals or groups. I noticed, for example, that the applause for Dr. Cobbs reached a higher volume of intensity than that received by any of the *white* speakers at this conference.

This is consistent with my hypothesis that in the entertainment field, all conditions being generally equal, black performers will usually receive somewhat more applause from *white* audiences than will white entertainers.

The facile explanation is, obviously, white guilt. But perhaps something more is involved. Perhaps such applause is one of the few gestures of goodwill that whites know how to make toward blacks. It isn't much, but it *is* something.

One of the most fascinating exchanges—as Dr. Freeman has reminded us—came when Dr. Cobbs characterized Dr. Park's concept of the ghettoization of prison populations as *shoddy*.

We do not have time here to take up the details of the controversy itself, but we might learn something from the nature of Dr. Park's response to Dr. Cobbs' verbal attack. *Your* response was not to gasp but to *smile*. Several of you, in fact, turned to *me* and smiled, as if to say, "Get a load of what's going on." I did.

But Dr. Park's response was primarily emotional, perhaps visceral, as evidenced by the immediate breakdown in his sentence structure. As the tape-recorded transcript will show, he communicated in various unconnected fragments of sentences for a few seconds and then counterattacked, not ad hominem but ad civita. What else might one expect, it occurred to Dr. Park to ask, from someone who lived in San Francisco?

It is certainly not my purpose here either to make light of Dr. Park or to force him to relive those few awkward moments during which egos were wounded and exposed.

My intention is rather to emphasize the frailty of our capacity for reason. Passion may occasionally inspire men to eloquence but it is more likely to render them less rather than more articulate and reasonable. Dr. Park, then, stands for every man. Perhaps none of us are truly graceful under surprise attack.

I was myself subjected to critical aspersions and had my loyalty questioned by a woman in the audience I addressed here locally on Friday at noon.

My response, too, was to feel a surge of emotion. It was

low level but its components were recognizable as fear and anger.

So we all carry this ancient animal burden, part protection and part curse. The knowledge should make us more charitable in dealing with those with whom we disagree.

Dr. Girvetz has become a typical figure in the contemporary American political drama, the liberal who, though he does not substantially change himself, feels the ground shift under him, as a result of which social earthquake he comes to rest at a point farther to the right on the political spectrum than he is accustomed to.

Today's liberal is historically symptomatic, however, in a sense that merits him far better treatment than the casual dismissal or outright contempt he sometimes receives from those to his left or those who feel that he has not done enough for them. For the values and institutions the liberal defends are those that were unknown for countless ages, those that were prayed for, dreamed for, struggled for, died for by a now-faceless mass of valiant souls who suffered under a thousand tyrannies and longed pathetically for the freedom to speak their minds, to write or otherwise disseminate their views, to travel without harsh restriction, to worship or not, as it pleased them, to congregate with others at will, to live in such social conditions that one could at least *pursue* happiness, insure domestic tranquility, and function as both reason and passion have told the best among us down through the ages man was meant to function.

The crimes of the Industrial Revolution rudely cut across these libertarian dreams. Clearly the people deserved a large measure of economic security. It is perhaps the primary task of this century to determine if the inherent contradiction between *freedom* on the one hand and *security* on the other can be reasonably balanced.

Even now the liberal stands between the Radical Left and the Radical Right, who might today be at each other's throats if it were not for his intervention.

The liberal is as open to criticism as everyone else, but

in concentrating on his shortcomings we must not lose sight of the herculean achievements of progressive forces over the centuries in advancing human freedom.

Speaking of freedom, a gentleman in the audience expressed a combination of horror and surprise that a recent survey shows that young children voted *against* our constitutional guarantees of liberty, against free speech, against legal rights, and so forth.

But I would have thought that children were recognized as notoriously intolerant. They are trained to *receive* love rather than to give it, to receive material necessities rather than to provide them to others. An infant is a squalling, screaming bundle of insistent demands, not a beneficent dispenser of blessings and concern for others.

Faced with the question as to how to deal with evildoers, children almost invariably recommend harsh punishment because they are motivated by their horror of the evil done, not by those sophisticated and tolerant standards which it took adult mankind untold hundreds of thousands of years to develop, and which even now are shakily buttressed by popular sentiment even in the most civilized societies.

Because of their exposure to TV and films, children incline to believe that the way to treat a bad man is to have Gary Cooper or John Wayne or Jack Webb shoot him on the spot. And they are not alone.

Dr. Bierer wisely draws our attention to the fact that on the one hand we have millions of wealthy or retired people who report that they have little to do to productively occupy their time, while on the other hand almost all necessary social agencies report a shortage of helpful workers. Clearly the idle personnel must somehow be directed toward the areas of need. Perhaps experienced management people, given the opportunity for public communication, could productively deal with this problem.

Something along this line is already being done by the *Thiokol Chemical Corporation*, for whom I recently narrated a documentary film telling of their very positive and productive program for training hard-core, unemployable young ghetto people, not only for regular jobs or further academic studies, but, perhaps most significantly, training them to do the same work by which they were helped so that they in turn can have a positive, productive feedback in their ghetto communities. This program deserves far more public attention than it has received and I recommend it to your further study.

I am troubled by a certain looseness of language which seems to me symptomatic of our time. In discussing *violence* yesterday one gentleman said "rats are violent." Others make the claim that poverty itself is violence upon the poor. Having lived with both poverty and with rats in my own youth, I know their ugliness. It is disgusting and disgraceful that people should have to live in rat-infested tenements. But to bend the word *violence* to cover this painful-enough reality, it seems to me, confuses rather than clarifies the issue.

In the debate on obscenity one hears it said that *war* is obscene, that *violence* is obscene. Words are imprecise enough to begin with, judged as scientific instruments, without our rendering them even more rubbery.

Lastly we were moved by Judge Lodge's recitation of his experience in visiting Atascadero State Hospital and finding that he was the only judge, out of over 500, who had accepted the inmates' invitation to attend a conference there.

Perhaps there is some connection between Judge Lodge's social conscience and his youth. Such men serve for me as yardsticks by which I measure my own passage through time. Partly I suppose because my health is still good I do not feel as old as I am, which is 49. But since I reached the middle thirties I began to notice the strange phenomenon that policemen were starting to look like high-school boys. Eventually clergymen, doctors, and now even judges look like college youths.

In closing, I take it that we would agree that there is no one magic answer, no one philosophical framework within which all problems will be resolved and all difficulties surmounted. Those abstractions, representing concrete enough realities, which elicit hope in our hearts—*education, religion, democracy, freedom, psychiatry, political constitutionalism*—even such attractive ideals are not panaceas.

Perhaps I should mention that I am a Christian so that you will understand my fundamental bias in regard to this question. I stand, in other words, among those who hold that religion in essence is a positive force and one capable of influencing human behavior in acceptable directions. But the fact remains that the pages of religious history are stained with such rivers and seas of human blood, that the record of religious practice is blackened by instances of such massive intolerance and fanaticism, that it cannot possibly be responsibly argued that religion pure and simple is *the* answer our hearts seek.

Nor can *education* be that answer. Germany in the 1930s was the best-educated nation in Europe. The German people were also highly religious, for that matter; at least they were affiliated with the various Christian churches. But this religious and well-educated people nevertheless perpetrated the horrors, under Hitler's guidance, that led to the massive destruction of World War II.

As for *freedom*, we feel its lack sensitively and its loss even more painfully. Obviously it is a good. But it frequently provides operative room in which countless moral atrocities and obscenities are committed.

It is not a proper response to such understanding to turn *against* education, religion, or freedom; we are merely advised against investing overly large amounts of hope in such conditions.

It is perhaps a wonder, or a tribute to our resourcefulness and resiliency, that we know any happiness or intellectual satisfaction at all, given that our existence is quite literally bounded by mystery and death.

Consider the two fundamental concepts by which we locate ourselves, *space* and *time*. Concerning each there are two possible positions, both of which are absurd. Either time began, which is preposterous, since we can easily think of a continuum *before* it began, or it did *not* begin, which we cannot think of at all. Either it will end or it will not, both of which are obviously impossible.

As for space, either it is infinite, which cannot be the case, or it ends somewhere, which is equally preposterous.

We are born ignorant animals and we die in pain and confusion. In between we can perceive and create things of beauty and value, but part of our tragedy is that they can all be turned to evil ends. Whether we speak of freedom, democracy, education, religion, courage, love, or sex, everything that we need to sustain us can also kill us; everything can be abused, as well as used.

This association merits great credit for its attempts to induce man to make the wisest possible use of his mental, spiritual, and material resources.

Chapter 11

Serving as Toastmaster

The Toastmaster's Function

The word *toastmaster* itself is not as commonly spoken at present as it was twenty-five or fifty years ago. In the old, pretelevision days the banquet program, complete with several after-dinner speeches, was a popular form of American entertainment. It was necessary for someone—usually an officer of the host organization—to serve as master of ceremonies to introduce the various speakers and other dignitaries. The word *toastmaster* comes, of course, from the word *toast*, meaning the little speech in which graceful words of praise are expressed: "To the ladies," "To His Majesty," "To dear old Harvard," or whatever. Toasts are rarely offered at large public dinners nowadays, although they are still common at more intimate personal gatherings.

If the fact cheers you, I have a slight speaker's block myself on what, to most people, is the easiest sort of public address of all, offering a toast. I suppose the fact that my social background is lower-middle-class Chicago Irish—a culture in which no toasts were ever spoken, although a lot of them were drunk—accounts for the fact that I never even heard a formal toast delivered until I was an adult. In any event, I've sometimes envied the social ease and grace with which some gentlemen—and, in recent years, ladies—leap to their feet after a pleasant dinner and offer a toast appropriate to the occasion.

The solution to my block? Simple. I just go ahead and do it anyway, whether I like it or not. And to this day no one has ever been aware that I've had any difficulty at the task. If toasts are a big deal in your social culture, you might want to check out a library book in which samples are included. Some speakers make a special art of this, memorizing jokes, poems, famous sayings of great figures of history, lyrics of songs, or whatever they consider useful. There's nothing wrong with that, either, although I've noticed that the most effective toasts are those which come from the heart. An example of such might be: "Well, friends, I can add only that this has been a delightful occasion—an evening characterized by friendship and warmth. But before we go our separate ways tonight it occurs to me that we ought to thank the women of the dinner committee, those unsung heroines without whom this lovely banquet could not have taken place at all. A toast, then, to these fine women."

Again, nothing that would top Winston Churchill—but perfectly suited, in style, to many an occasion.

Experienced toastmasters either prepare or have prepared for them separate cards on which are typed the various announcements and introductions a formal dinner requires. This takes more hard work than creativity, since there may be a dozen or so names and titles to announce. Those introduced will usually expect to hear a certain amount of flattery, or at least some sort of brief reference to their professional accomplishments.

You will be wise, however, to insist on one point: that the host group itself agree to provide you with the announcements in double-spaced typed form. Although such a request seems simple enough, it is often misunderstood. I have sometimes been given cards with dumb instructions like "Introduce the councilman." I generally don't even know who the councilman is, much less how to introduce him or her. Prewritten cards solve all such problems. You can, of course, add comments of your own.

One of your first and most important tasks as a toastmaster, you may be surprised to learn, is to make the audience shut up. You may have had long and vast experience in dealing with humans as individuals, but audiences are quite another breed of creature. People will often be guilty of incredible rudeness when part of an audience, to a degree that they would not dream of if alone in your company. Among the very worst audiences—and this, too, will no doubt come as a surprise—are wealthy people. Perhaps social power has a tendency to spoil those who possess it. They become used to having their own way, to taking no back talk from others, and in time this produces a certain degree of insensitivity. On the three instances over the years when I have seen an audience behave in a truly boorish fashion, they consisted entirely of well-to-do people, the power elite of the communities in question.

On the occasion, some years back, when I served as toastmaster at a St. Patrick's Day dinner at a swank hotel, I noticed that the audience continued to talk, laugh, clink dishware, and walk about all through a fifteen-minute performance by one of America's better-known vocalists. Even after the singing had ended, it took quite a bit of doing to bring silence to the room. A few minutes later I said, "You know, I've been trying to figure out exactly why this audience simply refused to shut up and listen to Dennis Day. It couldn't be that you didn't care for his singing, because he did a marvelous job and you gave him a well-deserved ovation when he had finished. It certainly couldn't be because you are Irish, because I have attended other functions with Irish audiences that were completely respectful. Well, I've finally figured out what it was. It's because you're rich, and you're just not used to taking any guff from anybody."

On another occasion an audience misbehaved outrageously for a full three hours. The men present were about three hundred owners and managers of television stations affiliated with one of America's major networks. The women were their wives. They paid no attention whatever to a dozen famous TV entertainers, none of whom were being paid a penny to perform for them.

The third instance occurred some years ago when I was serving as the host of the *Tonight* show. In those days, even when the program was telecast live, we frequently originated it not from our regular New York studios but from other cities around the country. A large community in northern New York state which I shall not identify had invited us to do the show one evening under their auspices; the invitation was accepted. It was, of course, necessary to report to the scene of the program two or three days early. On the night before the telecast, all the members of our party—among whom were singers Andy Williams, Pat Kirby, Steve Lawrence, and Eydie Gorme, announcer Gene Rayburn, and orchestra leader Skitch Henderson—were treated to a dinner with formal remarks, entertainment, and dancing at a local country club. To this day I cannot understand why our hosts acted as they did.

About 90 percent of them very quickly got drunk as skunks. This was, in a sense, their right and would not now be mentioned were it not that their stupor had unfortunate effects on the rest of us. A good many of the men present—civic and business leaders— seemed to feel that they were entitled to paw the women in our company. Their wives, on their part, were not averse to flirting with the male members of our group. During the entertainment that took place, the noise the audience was making pretty well drowned out the pitiful attempts of a singer and master of ceremonies to compete. Some of our hosts argued, loudly and abusively, with each other. Most of us connected with the *Tonight* program at that time were in our twenties and thirties. All of us were shocked by what we witnessed.

I'm sorry to report that there is no simple solution to this problem. When I am still seated and someone else is serving as toastmaster, I always try to help her or him through such difficult moments by turning my head upstage and shushing—as loudly as possible— for several seconds. I'm usually joined in this by other keepers of the peace who are disturbed at the rudeness of those around them, and our combined effort usually does the trick.

Tapping on the microphone or clinking a spoon against a glass of water also helps. Sometimes, though, nothing helps, and you're simply in for a rough time. There was a time in our country when

social manners were considered of great importance by almost everyone except the poorly trained and educated. That time, one regrets
to observe, would appear to be long past.

Whatever you do at such moments, there's no point in adding
your own rudeness to that of the audience. You are, after all, not
an animal tamer, who can dominate by the power of personal
magnetism or physical threat. Keep a smile on your face, however
insincere, do the best you can to restore order, and hurry along.

You might want to use a line something like an ad-lib that
occurred to me one night when, at an unruly moment, a member
of the audience called out, "Sss-hhhhhh! *Quiet!*"

Pretending to believe that the admonition was addressed to me,
I said, "I'm sorry; I'm speaking as quietly as I can."

As toastmaster you will also have to announce the national
anthem and introduce the member of the clergy delivering the
invocation, if there is one. You will be expected to be at least
moderately witty. You will be responsible for seeing to it that the
program adheres, at least approximately, to the time schedule, and
at the end you will be expected to bring the proceedings to a graceful
conclusion.

Your introductions, even to your chief speakers, need not be
outrageously flowery and emotional; neither should they be too casual
or offhand. If humans were fully rational animals they would not
require such constant instruction, but the fact is that you have to
keep telling people things again and again. Even then you need not
expect that your full message will be absorbed, much less properly
recalled if it is. Therefore, even though you may imagine that your
guest speaker is so famous as to "need no introduction," you should
give him or her one anyway, referring at least to the high points of
his or her illustrious career.

After you have made your introductions you should attend carefully to what the other speakers say and do. This will give you the
opportunity to make a few appropriate spontaneous comments when
they have finished.

Also, listening attentively to a speaker requires you to look at
her or him—partly a matter of applying the Golden Rule anyway—

which is exactly what you would want a toastmaster to do if you were speaking. The speaker will probably direct a few remarks to you personally, and if at such times you are tying your shoelace, whispering to the person next to you, or otherwise inattentive, the audience will notice the breakdown in communication.

When the speaker finishes his or her remarks, stand up at once and vigorously lead the applause. You need not, at such moments, make any extended commentary on the speech just concluded, but you should say something about it, naturally of a complimentary or humorous nature.

If you are reasonably well known to at least most of those present, it will not be necessary that you, as toastmaster, be introduced. If you are a stranger, then of course some local dignitary will be required to introduce you.

At the conclusion of the evening your last task will be to let the audience know that the proceedings have been finished and that all present may go home. Failure to attend to this seemingly minor detail will end the program on something of a faltering note.

Organizing a Benefit Program

After you have served as toastmaster for several dinner programs, it will begin to occur to you that you know more about how they should be conducted than the people organizing them, and you will shortly perceive the wisdom of cooperating with the planning committee in organizing a program.

One thing to look out for: If there is entertainment in addition to speeches, be certain that both the performers and the committee have a sharply defined understanding of how much time may be devoted to each individual turn. I have seen more than a few dinners spoiled because a singer who should have done only two or three songs proceeded to do six or seven.

If there are several speakers, they too should understand that there are time limitations on the various portions of the program. It may not seem terribly important if just one speaker rambles on for six or seven minutes longer than the allotted time, but if several do so, whoever closes the program will have a very difficult time of it. The audience would be in no mood, that late in the evening, to give even Lincoln a warm reception if he were to return from the grave and redeliver the Gettysburg Address.

Do not be surprised if one detail or another—or perhaps even a few of them—are botched up. This is not unusual; it is par for the course.

I still recall the time I attended a benefit at the Waldorf-Astoria Hotel in New York City. The cause was a worthy one and the evening was, by and large, a success. Notables sat at every table, and the dais was lined with dignitaries. Almost fifteen hundred paying guests were crammed into the grand ballroom, gladdening the treasurer's heart and swelling the organization's coffers. Eddie Cantor addressed the assemblage, as did George Jessel, Postmaster Jim Farley, Harry Hershfield, Milton Berle, and several other celebrities.

The next morning, however, *Variety* reported that whoever planned the program had slighted Milton Berle by relegating him to a last-minute, anticlimactic position, and that "Mr. Television" had gotten a little hot under the collar and stalked from the room in a huff after his brief address.

As a benefit veteran, angry or not, Milton couldn't have been too surprised. Perhaps his plight might have called to mind the story of the great blow that Dr. Robert A. Millikan struck, just a year earlier, for all long-suffering after-dinner speakers.

The famed scientist, well into his eighties, waited through more than three hours of preliminaries to give a speech at a Chamber of Commerce dinner in Van Nuys, California. Finally, near midnight, after the audience had grown glassy-eyed from talk, talk, talk, Millikan arose and said, "At this hour, I fear the mind is too weary to listen to the speech I have prepared. I had intended to discuss one of the chapters of my new book, *The Road to Peace*. Any of you who are interested may read the book."

The stunned silence that followed must have warmed the cockles of Millikan's heart. He had, bless him, done something that all professional after-dinner speakers and entertainers have been itching to do for years: gotten back in the simplest and most effective way at the individual whose stupidity had been responsible for such a poorly planned program.

An isolated instance? Not at all. I was invited to entertain, during World War II, at a dinner given for the graduating class of an Arizona training field for Chinese airmen.

It was during the war and Uncle Sam, busy making flyers out of young Chinese recruits, was aware of his obligation to provide them with entertainment and wholesome recreation. Unfortunately, in the process of trying to amuse them, I suffered the torture that only a comedian can feel when he discovers that his audience does not find him particularly amusing. It was not until I had retired from the stage in embarrassment that the jovial colonel who had engaged me for the evening told me the reason the boys hadn't laughed at my jokes.

"You see," he explained, "they don't speak English!"

Every performer could tell dozens of such stories. As a matter of fact, few of us who are regularly called upon to entertain gratis can recall many instances in which the wheels of a benefit program have been oiled with enough care to ensure that the show ran smoothly from beginning to end.

Rules for Planning a Program

In the hope that this book will come to the attention of the program chairman of at least a few organizations planning to organize banquet-hall extravaganzas, I submit a few general rules which, if followed, will not only make life more pleasant for the entertainers involved, but will add to the audience's enjoyment.

1. Work well in advance. Contact the performers you're trying to book early enough to enable both parties to work the engagement into their schedules. There's another good reason for planning ahead: Sometimes celebrities just can't fulfill their promises to appear at your affair, and they won't feel so guilty about it if they can give you two or three weeks' warning.

2. Approach performers by mail or through their publicity representatives; don't buttonhole them in restaurants. In your first letter explain the purpose of the dinner, dance, or show you're planning and give a general outline of the way in which the performer can help your cause by making an appearance.

3. If your invitation is accepted, send another letter giving exact and important details: time, place, address, size of audience, type of affair (basketball rally? funeral? church social? variety show?), type of attire suitable, and the individual's position on the program. This last is tremendously important. When a performer is told to arrive promptly at 8 o'clock because "that's the time the show starts," and then doesn't go on until 11:45, he's rarely in a happy frame of mind by the time he goes out on the stage.

   Tell your guest what time the entertainment will get under way, then give a separate time by which he or she must be on hand. Your guests may surprise you and spend the whole evening with your group, but if a busy schedule makes things difficult, they can take advantage of those extra hours.

4. Be certain you have a microphone and public address system that is functioning properly if you feel amplifying equipment is necessary, which it almost always is. Don't stage a show in an auditorium with poor acoustics. I recall the time a dozen performers and I wasted an entire evening trying to entertain several thousand people in a New Jersey armory. Reason: They couldn't understand a word that was said, because each sound wave boomed and rattled around inside the giant cavern like a peanut in a boxcar.

5. Try not to combine a floor show with a dance. Dance crowds are usually noisy and hard to handle, seating arrangements can be awkward, and dance-hall acoustics are, more often than not, inadequate.

6. When lining up talent, try for a balanced program. I once emceed a show at an army camp and finally ran out of ways

to introduce vocalists. The program chairman had invited one comic and eight singers. The last few met with a cold response, to put it mildly.

7. By all means have a frank discussion with your talent about encores. If a true star is on, the audience can stand three or four encores; but if that up-and-coming singer Joe Nobody is at the mike, get it over with as quickly as possible. The problem is simply one of time. The best audiences in the world will cool off if a show drags on, no matter how great the talent is. Performers won't be offended if you tell them that the show is a little long and the janitor has to come in at midnight. Of course, there's a better solution: Don't overload the program with acts.

When Things Go Wrong

Despite the combined best efforts of a program committee and a toastmaster, there are occasional evenings which seem to have been cursed. I recall the time several years ago that officers of UNICO, an Italian-American organization, decided to arrange an important banquet in Los Angeles to honor the great songwriter Harry Warren, composer of such hits as "I Only Have Eyes for You," "You're Getting to Be a Habit with Me," "42nd Street," "You're My Everything," "The Lullaby of Broadway," "Jeepers Creepers," and "Chattanooga Choo Choo."

I was first alerted to the forthcoming event when I received a call from my good friend Gus Bivona, a clarinetist and bandleader. He had just been hired to provide the orchestra for the affair.

"The whole thing will be to honor Harry Warren," Gus said, "and some of the UNICO guys said that because you're a composer yourself, and you love good music, you'd be right to emcee the show."

"I'd love to," I said, and asked to be provided with further details.

A few days later a letter arrived, giving the names of speakers, entertainers, and local dignitaries who would be participating. I was asked if I could recommend any suitable entertainment. The only idea that occurred to me was to book my dear friends, comedians

Bill Dana and Pat Harrington, Jr. The reason these particular names came to mind—as opposed to, for example, those of Louis Nye and Don Knotts, who also worked on my television show at the time—was that a few weeks earlier Bill and Pat had done a comedy record album for a company in which I had a financial interest. The funniest routine on the album was Pat Harrington's portrayal of a character called Guido Panzini, who, it was alleged, had been first mate of the ill-fated *Andrea Doria*, the Italian liner that had been involved in an accident at sea some months earlier. It may be recalled that a few members of the Italian crew had not exactly distinguished themselves when, instead of shepherding the women and children into the ship's lifeboats, they first made certain of their own security. As I recall, only a few men out of a large crew were guilty of such conduct, but as is often the case it was the negative part of the story which made an impression on the public consciousness.

In retrospect, it was easy to see that recommending to Pat and Bill that they do the *Andrea Doria* bit at an all-Italian dinner was not the wisest suggestion I ever made. It occurred to me, however, because when one is putting a show together, preexisting comedy routines or monologues that have some relation to the subject matter at hand are often the first straws for which one clutches. If one were booking attractions for a football banquet, for example, it would be natural to ask Andy Griffith to do his famous football monologue, to ask Don Adams if he would do his funny routine about football cheers, or to ask Tim Conway if he would perform his marvelous comedy interview in which he plays a harebrained road manager for a professional team.

In this case my reasoning was simple. It's an Italian dinner; let's see, who do I know who does an Italian routine?

The banquet was held in the large ballroom of the then-new and glamorous Beverly Hilton Hotel in Beverly Hills, California. As I mingled with the crowd during the cocktail hour, I began to pick up comments that indicated there might be some confusion about the evening. A number of people were overheard to ask just who Harry Warren was, and two or three who knew him fairly well still seemed puzzled that he had been chosen to be the guest of honor at such an illustrious outing; they thought he was Jewish.

Eventually the audience assumed dinner places and the waiters began to serve a sumptuous meal. The first indication that the evening had already taken a peculiar turn was when it suddenly occurred to me that the dinner serenade I had been listening to for perhaps a quarter of an hour consisted, not of Harry Warren's music, but of my own.

During the orchestra's first intermission I excused myself from the head table and sauntered over to Gus, who was just stepping off the bandstand.

"Thanks a million for playing my tunes, man," I said, "but do you plan to play anything by Harry Warren?"

"Well," he said, "not during the dinner hour. I just brought charts of those twelve songs of yours that we did in the new album. To tell you the truth, I didn't give the thing much thought."

Bivona had indeed recorded a dozen of my songs a few weeks earlier, the arrangements having been done by Henry Mancini and Skip Martin, an arranger for the Les Brown orchestra. Gus and I both assumed, of course, that during the formal entertainment later in the evening heavy emphasis would be put on Warren's music. I returned to the head table, and for the next forty-five minutes or so continued to enjoy the orchestra's melodious and spirited renditions of my own compositions. The exclusive playing of them must, I suppose, have greatly puzzled Harry Warren, who had been assured that every part of the evening's festivities was intended as a tribute to him that was not only well deserved, but for which the poor man had been waiting during some thirty years of general obscurity.

At last the dinner had been served, the waiters had removed the dishes, and it was time to get to the program itself.

When one serves as a master of ceremonies for an affair of this sort, one is provided with cards on which are typed introductions to the various program participants. The order in which the various ladies and gentlemen appear, either to speak or to entertain, is predetermined; the introductions therefore are rendered in the appropriate order. The first gentleman I was called upon to introduce was a Catholic priest. His name escapes me, but he was a pastor at a local church, perhaps the one attended by Mr. Warren, who—contrary to common assumption, even in the music business—was not Jewish but Italian Catholic.

The priest was seated about a dozen chairs to my left, and when I introduced him I naturally assumed that he would take over my microphone at the center of the head table, offer the customary brief invocation, and return to his seat. To this day I haven't the slightest idea why he kept on walking when he reached the podium. He did not stop until, a good two minutes later, he reached a microphone at the far side of the room—in right field, so to speak—in front of the orchestra, on a small dance floor. Two thousand pairs of eyes followed his peculiar journey through the room, which he accomplished by curving around tables, bumping a shoulder or two, and all in all having a bit of difficulty wending his way to the distant mike.

Eventually he reached it and, one assumes, muttered a suitable prayer. I say "assumes," because the microphone was not turned on, nor is there any reason why it should have been; the audio engineer had expected that the good father would speak into the mike designated for his use. No one in the room, with the possible exception of a few people standing very close to him, will ever know what he said. There would be no evidence that he said anything at all except that his lips were observed to move. His prayer made such a faint impression on the audience that I would not be surprised to learn that God himself, no doubt being otherwise occupied at the time, overlooked it.

And, of course, after the pastor had finished his mumbled remarks, all guests—still standing respectfully—had then to wait while he retraced his long, rambling course back to his chair. A number of witty comments occurred to me, but I held my tongue.

When the priest had returned to his starting place, I made the traditional announcement, "And now, ladies and gentlemen, the national anthem." At this point dazzling spotlights, properly enough, focused on an American flag behind the dais down to my right. As it happened, a short, thin gentleman named Ned Washington, himself the lyricist of a number of fine popular songs over the years, was standing directly in front of the flag. Washington had no idea, however, that Old Glory was behind him. All he knew was that he alone, out of two thousand people, was suddenly illuminated by two of the brightest spotlights he had ever seen. His face, as he tried to fathom why this might be so, was a study. He blinked, smiled, looked from side to side in embarrassment, frowned, looked at me, raised his eyebrows, and blinked once more into the lights. Most of us, of course, were singing, but a number of people, observing Washington's puzzlement, blew a few notes, and there was a bit of elbowing and giggling, I regret to say, during the singing of the anthem.

Pat Harrington has recalled, "I was next to Ned and also partly blinded by the spot on the flag. I estimate the flag and stand at five feet, three inches, and Ned is about five feet, five inches, so he covered it completely. He hadn't been paying attention to the announcements and stood up perfunctorily when everyone else did. When the spot hit the flag—or him—he froze, thinking he had been singled out for some momentary praise. When he heard the first words of the anthem coming up from the crowd, he side-mouthed to me, 'I didn't write this.' "

I then formally welcomed the audience and opened the evening with a few jokes.

Another tip-off that things were not going to go well came after I had introduced the first of several civic dignitaries representing, respectively, the county and city of Los Angeles and the state of California. Two of these gentlemen, in fulsomely praising Mr. Warren, and asserting the enormous respect in which he was held by millions of Californians, referred to him quite distinctly as Harry Warner.

The first time this happened the audience gasped, then laughed. I leaped to my feet, stepped briefly to the microphone, and said, "No, no, Mr. Simpkins. The dinner for Harry *Warner* is taking place in the ballroom on the *other* side of the lobby."

This saved the moment, in a sense, although I'm sure it did not relieve the speaker's embarrassment. It seemed to put him, in fact, in something of a panic, so that a moment or two later he concluded his remarks by saying, "And therefore it gives me great pleasure indeed to present this handsome plaque, from the people of Los Angeles and the mayor personally, to that great American composer, Harry *Warner*."

It was the coliseum roar of laughter that greeted the second gaffe that probably unsettled the nerves of the following speaker. I can think of no other explanation as to why he would get up and commit exactly the same offense, but he did.

It was then time to introduce the first entertainer of the evening, a young gentleman of whom I had never heard before, nor since. His name was Joe Vina. I said something to the effect that it was remarkable how many of America's greatest singers over the years were Italian and that I had every confidence that young Joe Vina was going to join the distinguished company of Frank Sinatra, Dean Martin, Enrico Caruso, Perry Como, Russ Columbo, et al.

Just as I was about to call for the usual "nice big hand" for Vina, my eyes drifted to the orchestra. Far from being on the qui vive, instruments poised, the musicians were lounging about in their chairs. Most of them were not holding instruments at all, and were clearly in a state of nonattention. While I had no idea what the explanation of this mysterious circumstance might be, neither did I have the luxury of speculating about it, so I simply introduced Vina. He promptly ran out, smiled broadly, waited until the applause died down, spread his arms wide as if he were about to leap off a rocky cliff on the west coast of Mexico, and then—believe it or not—just stood there with his mouth open, not making a sound.

Two thousand people stared at this puzzling spectacle for a few seconds. My eyes went again to Bivona and his orchestra, none of whom yet gave any indication that they were expected to accompany Mr. Vina. In an instant I solved the mystery and rose to my feet.

"Joe," I said, "by the fact that the orchestra hasn't snapped to attention may I assume that you had planned to do a record-synch?"

"Yes, Mr. Allen," he called out gratefully. "They're supposed to play my record now."

"Well, thank you, Joe," I said. "I guess whoever the engineer is now knows what he's supposed to do, so don't you worry about a thing, Joe. We're all with you, and I'm sure we'll enjoy hearing your recording, whatever it turns out to be. We'll also be impressed, I'm sure, by your singing live right along with it, if that's part of your plan."

Inasmuch as I had already made it clear that we were gathered for the purpose of honoring Harry Warren and his truly incredible contributions to American music, it was naturally assumed that whatever number Vina had recorded was one written by Harry. No such luck, of course. The record finally started—much too loud, as I recall. Vina had a bit of trouble synchronizing his motions with it, but finally he and the record were on the same track. The number had a faintly Italian flavor, as I recall, but naturally fell strangely on the ears of Harry Warren, who no doubt also had assumed that Vina was there to accord him the honor of performing one of his songs.

After Vina had retired from the stage-dance floor, I introduced a young lady named Pat Healy who, it was anticipated, would regale us with not one, but a medley of songs by Harry Warren. The spotlight illuminated the location where it was reasonable to look for Miss Healy, but she did not appear. I jumped up again to the dais mike and began a verbal search for the missing singer. The light roamed around a bit while again Bivona and the orchestra sat with the same degree of interest and curiosity as the audience, not preparing to play their instruments but simply craning their necks to locate Miss Healy. She was finally found, oddly enough, lost in thought, seated at a nearby table, from which dreamily—and unsteadily—she arose and moved to the microphone.

I never had the pleasure of getting to know Miss Healy well, so to this day I do not know whether she had a few drinks too many or whether she simply had one of those loose, off-the-cuff personalities that, a few years later, were to become associated with the hippy demeanor.

"Oh, wow," she said, running a hand through her already disordered hair. "I'm not really dressed for the occasion and I'm sorry to say I-I—haven't prepared a particular song. In fact, I don't know what to sing at *all*."

Two thousand jaws dropped.

I looked at Harry Warren and groaned inwardly.

"Please, God," I said to myself, "whatever the hell she sings let it be something written by this great composer."

"Well," Miss Healy continued, "I mean, I didn't bring any arrangements with me—as a matter of fact, I don't *have* any arrangements of anything written by Mr. Warren, so maybe the piano player and the drummer and I can, you know, just *fake* a little something here, to pay our respects to Harry—er—Warren."

Miss Healy's approach might have been defensible if she had not the slightest warning that she was about to be called upon, but to my knowledge she had had a good many days' warning.

"What would you folks like to hear?" she said, not very wisely.

Somebody called out, "How about 'Lullaby of Broadway'?" one of Warren's great standards.

"All right," she said, at which she turned to the drummer and indicated, by languidly waving her hand, at what tempo she wanted to do the number.

As anyone over twenty will know, "Lullaby of Broadway" is one of the best up-tempo numbers ever written, very much on a par with the best of Gershwin, Porter, or Berlin. It is peppy, original, harmonically complex, and yet eminently singable. Nevertheless, although you may find it hard to believe, Miss Healy indicated to the drummer and pianist a tempo that would have been more suitable for "Someone to Watch over Me." Perhaps the word *lullaby* had confused her.

The musicians had no alternative but to play an introduction in her snaillike tempo. She sang—not precisely on key, either— "Come . . . on . . . along . . . and . . . listen . . . tooo . . . the . . . lull . . . ah . . . by . . . of . . . Broad . . . way."

Mercifully, considering possible alternatives, she proceeded at once to forget the rest of the lyric and then said, "Oh, God, I forget the words. Mr. Warren, can you ever *forgive* me?"

We all know the answer to that question.

"God," she said, "I'm so sorry. This is really embarrassing. I'll tell you what—I'll make up for it, Mr. Warren, by doing *another* one of your great songs. This is one my *mother* used to sing to me. Actually, my mother should be here tonight, because she was a lot better singer than I am. She was really *great*, my mother was. Let's

see, now . . . what was it I was going to sing, anyway? Harry Warren, please *help* me!"

By this time the audience had lost control and was laughing. It
was not actually a cruel laughter and was not really directed at Miss
Healy herself. The object of the laughter was simply the astounding
incongruity of the situation. On the one hand was one of America's
greatest composers, and on the other incredible long-playing chaos
that was supposed to have been a tribute to him.

I stepped to the microphone and said, "Well, Miss Healy, just
relax. Perhaps a little later in the evening the full lyrics to some
Harry Warren songs might occur to you."

She left the floor and, I would not be surprised to learn, show
business.

I felt that since the audience was already laughing this might
be a suitable time to introduce Pat Harrington and Bill Dana.

"Ladies and gentlemen," I said, "we are very honored to have
with us tonight a gentleman who is the cultural attaché to the United
States from the Italian government. He has recently come here from
Rome, and I know that you will want to hear his comments on this
marvelous evening staged under the auspices of UNICO."

At this stage in his career Bill Dana had not yet made his great
splash on our TV show as the lovable Mexican character Jose Ji-
menez. He had worked chiefly, to this date, as a comedy writer. He
has one of those swarthy Mediterranean faces that could pass for
Jewish, Greek, Spanish, or—in this instance—Italian.

Bill, as the Italian diplomat, stepped to the mike, thanked me,
and said, "Good-a evening, ladies and a-gentlemen. I'm glad to
introduce-a to you tonight-a a man who was a survivor of the crash
at sea between-a the *Andrea Doria* and-a the *Stockholm*. He's-a here
with-a me now."

Pat stepped to the mike.

"Sir, did you come over with the *Andrea Doria*?"

"Ala-most," Pat said.

"And what-a was your-a particular job?"

"My name is Guido Panzini. I'm Italian."

"Well, that's okay. Now, tell-a me, Mr. Panzini, what-a was
your job-a on the *Andrea Doria*?"

"I was the general officer. We had a young-a ladies on board. My job was to—"

"No, no. I mean-a, what was your *position?*"

"Are-a you kidding?"

The audience was laughing heartily.

"No, seriously, Officer Panzini, I want to ask-a you about the accident. When did you first-a realize you were on a collision course?"

"Well, it was when Captain Calamai asked a question—and-a somebody answered in Swedish."

"I see. And what was the first thing out of Captain Calamai's mouth?"

"When he realized what had happened?"

"Yes."

"His lunch."

"No, what I mean is . . . what was the first thing he *said?*"

"He said a beautiful, quaint old Italian expression."

"What was it?"

"Ma canso care mia fino—"

"And what does that mean?"

"It means *What did we hit down there?* At least, that is what it means in one dialect. In another dialect it means *Abandon ship!*"

"Talking about abandoning ship," Bill said, "there were a few rumors that the *crew* actually saw fit-a to abandon ship first."

"Well, that's only a *rumor.*"

"Is it true?"

"Yes, it's a *true* rumor. But you must understand-a the reason-a why it was that way. The passengers, they was-a too busy to get off the ship. They all went downstairs to take the snap-a shots of the accident, you know? Meanwhile, *we* got off the boat. I was way up on the bridge. I don't-a want to boast or anything, but I made it to the first life-a boat in 9.6. It's-a incredible. I finished-a second."

"Who finished-a first?"

"Captain Calamai did. He made it in 9.4."

Pat and Bill had gotten about this far into the routine when a remarkable thing happened. Far down to the left on the dais, perhaps a dozen seats or so away from the lectern, a short dark-complexioned man suddenly stood up and began walking toward us. At first I did not notice him, but then I saw that the people in the audience were no longer looking at Pat or Bill but were following a moving object to our left. When I turned to see what it might be, I observed a fellow whose face was red with fury and whose brows were knotted in a fierce scowl. During the three or four seconds before he reached the lectern my mental computer began to range over a number of possible explanations for the intrusion.

The man stomped angrily past us, muttering furiously under his breath in what, as I recall, was half-Italian and half-English. The only phrase I remember clearly was "You think-a it's-a funny, eh?"

Continuing his rightward progress, he approached a middle-aged woman seated far down to the other side, grabbed her by the wrist, pulled her to her feet, and, one assumes, said to her, "We're getting the hell out of here right now."

By this time Pat and Bill had, understandably enough, fallen into stupefied silence. The three of us joined the audience in simply staring at this peculiar demonstration, which now continued as the man and woman—he still furious, she looking puzzled and embarrassed—came back toward us. I thought that perhaps this time he might explain to us what was going on, and then it occurred to me that he might be a physician who had to leave to attend some emergency.

No such luck.

Pat Harrington recalls, "The guy stopped on the way back—with wife in tow—shouldered in between Bill and me, and said, 'This is not funny. People died, men were killed— This was a bad thing and you should not laugh.' He left, and when he got perhaps twenty feet away—still pulling his wife—Bill said, 'Boy, you know, you give a guy one line—one small line—and he thinks he's the whole act.'

"It got a laugh. I, of course, was frozen; the *Doria* was my piece, and for it to provoke this kind of reaction meant an unpardonable lack of sensibility on my part. Bill was trying to pull us out, I was stricken with onrushing guilt, and you, as I recall, were misting your fingernails."

The intruder now continued off to the left and then through a dozen or so tables, whose puzzled occupants stared at him open-mouthed.

The single oddest event in this whole crazy night occurred now. The lighting man was responsible for it. Apparently, observing from his distant perch at the other end of the great hall that three popular television comedians named Dana, Harrington, and Allen were at the lectern, he must have assumed that the stranger and his woman companion were part of the act. Accordingly, he had hit the man with a brilliant spotlight almost as soon as he had started to walk, and he and his assistant then continued to illuminate the two strangers, with *separate* spots, as they departed. This left Bill, Pat, and I in relative darkness, a factor for which we were at the moment profoundly grateful.

While the audience's attention was still focused on the man and his hapless wife I leaned over to one of the UNICO executives at the dais and said, "Who the hell were those people?"

"I'm sorry to tell you," the man said, "that he is what you said Bill Dana was. He's connected with the Italian Embassy—either here or in Washington, I'm not sure which."

The mystery about the man's anger was thereby explained. Although jokes about the *Andrea Doria* were funny to Americans, even those of Italian descent, to a representative of the Italian government the humor was not so readily apparent, particularly since some of the funniest jokes dealt with the cowardice of a few of the ship's crew.

It was, of course, out of the question for Bill and Pat to continue with the routine. Bill turned to me—speaking now without an accent—and said, "Steve, Pat and I would like to thank you very much for getting us into this thing tonight. Believe me, we'll remember this for a long time."

In a daze myself, I rose, thanked the fellows for being "good sports," whatever that meant, and explained, in case there were any other native Italians in the room, that there had been no intention to malign the Italian people nor to transgress the bounds of good taste in any way.

The next of several performers on the program—not a single

one of them celebrities, by the way—where were Frank Sinatra, Dean Martin, and Vic Damone?—was a young chap named Johnny Holiday. He is a fine singer, but I do think it would have been more appropriate if the dais had been graced by Tony Bennett, Buddy Greco, or Perry Como, not to mention an Italian comedian or two. But no, the singers present were all totally unknown to the public and, with the exception of the luckless Mr. Vina, were mostly non-Italians.

As for Mr. Holiday, the world will little note nor long remember what number he performed at this point, with the assistance of Gus Bivona and the orchestra, for the reason that the entire room was in noisy consternation over the dramatic walkout of the Italian diplomat and his wife.

A sotto-voce explanation of the incident started out from the dais, and as of five or six minutes later had reached the back of the room. This was accompanied, of course, by a rushing wave of whispers, hoarse cries, laughter, and catcalls. At any given moment hundreds of people were saying, "Who was that? What the hell's going on?" while those who had already absorbed the news were explaining the situation.

This inevitable wave of primitive communication did serve the purpose of apprising the audience of the benumbing state of affairs, but of course made it impossible to hear the song that was, all during this time, being sung by the unfortunate Holiday. If I am any judge of horseflesh, he too was singing something not written by Harry Warren; but, as I say, we will never know. Both music and lyrics were totally drowned out from start to finish.

Frequently, when audiences get even a little out of hand, the master of ceremonies takes over the microphone and either pleasantly or sharply calls for order. In this case I could not even do that much, since Holiday was singing—or reciting the Gettysburg Address, for all the evidence there was to the contrary.

At staggeringly long last, the evening drew to a close. The President of UNICO himself stepped to the lectern to make a presentation of the Italian-American group's most prestigious honor, called the Columbus Award. In presenting it the gentleman said, "It gives me great pleasure to present this handsome plaque to Harry Warner—er, *Warren*—because we are very proud of what he has accomplished in the world of music. And therefore, on behalf of UNICO, I present him the Columbus Award. Although it's not Columbus Day now, it will be next year."

More hysterical laughter.

I would not be surprised to learn that at least one of the handsome plaques that the guest of honor received that night is inscribed in bronze to Harry Warner.

One more thing: A couple of weeks later Gus Bivona and the members of his orchestra received their checks for playing at the event.

They bounced.

Chapter 12

Speaking on Radio and Television Talk Shows

It is conceivable that if you become effective as a speaker, and particularly if the messages you convey are also expressed in the form of magazine articles or books, you might eventually find yourself interviewed on radio or television.

One should be realistic about this aspect of your budding career as a lecturer, of course. It is extremely unlikely that you will receive urgent calls from the *Tonight* show or Ted Koppel's *Nightline* requesting your services as guest, although such adventures are not totally out of the question. But if you are interviewed by the media, it really won't matter whether your interrogator is Johnny Carson or some local radio personality in Paducah, Kentucky. You should, in either event, speak in as natural a manner as possible.

The style you have painstakingly developed for lectures is unlikely to be quite right when you are responding to an interviewer's questions. The typical talk-show style of speech, however, is not anything you need to study, since you've been doing it all your life.

Rule 1. Act naturally. If talking on the air doesn't seem to come naturally, then try pretending that the interview is taking place, not on radio or television, but on a park bench or in a rowboat. In such casual, comfortable settings, you certainly would not declaim like a great orator, project to the last row, or speak in a particularly forceful manner.

Rule 2.   Listen carefully to the questions. Do not, for example, make the common mistake of starting to respond to what you think the questioner will have asked when he finishes his or her question.

Also, you don't want to interrupt the interviewer, for two reasons. First, interrupting, particularly if it is repeated, will make you appear rude. Second, until the host has completed a question, you will not be sure how it will turn out.

Rule 3.   Don't ramble. The only real problem you might face on a talk show on which several guests are interviewed is trying to condense your message to the point where it can be expressed in just five or six minutes, since that is probably all that will be allotted to you.

The time to find out how many minutes you will be granted is, of course, before the program starts, not while you're on the air. This will be particularly true if your interview is to be run on a local newscast. Even presidents, popes, secretaries of state, and other dignitaries are usually shown making statements that last only a few seconds, obviously because a given thirty-minute newscast will be trying to cover news of importance all over the world, across the nation, in your state and, lastly, in the local community.

You would be well advised, therefore, to give your answers in short sentences. There's nothing you can do about editorial decisions made in the cutting room, and you ought not to be surprised if the most fascinating, pungent comments you make never get on the air at all, whereas the news editors may decide to carry some less interesting or even innocuous remark. While it does not totally justify such klutzy decisions, putting a newscast together is a job for which there never seems to be enough time. Consequently, snap decisions are made and, as is often the case in such settings, are not always for the best.

You should strive to concentrate on the factors that you *can* control. The practicing-aloud-in-the-car exercises will then have been helpful. Senator Edward M. Kennedy first ran into heavy weather during his 1980 campaign for the Democratic presidential nomination when it became apparent, from some of his informal television interviews, that he was less articulate than had theretofore been assumed. Words such as *inarticulate, indecisive,* and *faltering* were used to describe his methods of responding to questions at the time. The problem was by no means limited to the obviously awkward subject of the Chappaquiddick tragedy. Thomas Patterson, a political science professor at Syracuse University who had made a study of voter behavior during election periods, said of Kennedy's confrontation with Roger Mudd of CBS-TV: "The news isn't how Kennedy handles Chappaquiddick. The news is *how he's handling questions on TV about Chappaquiddick.* It creates a whole new issue." [Italics added.]

Rule 4. Think ahead. A study of Kennedy's difficulties in responding to unexpected questions, by Barry Siegel and Eleanor Randolf of *The Los Angeles Times,* quoted unidentified special consultants who suggested that the first commandment for television appearances is to anticipate all questions and prepare concise answers. And never to get "caught thinking about an answer while before the camera."

Having had experience in responding to questions, I differ with the last point. There's nothing wrong at all with being observed thinking about an answer. But of course you can't hem, haw, and digress. And if you can't think fast, then you would indeed be well advised to do as much preparation beforehand as possible.

Rule 5. Rehearse. If you have a helpful secretary, family member, or friend, you can check out your own abilities in a press conference setting by simply having one or more of them put a series of questions to you, in the privacy of your own home or office, just to see how well you respond. You might stand before a mirror while answering, or make a tape recording of your answers and listen to them later. Do you have the "uh—uh—" problem that troubles so many speakers? Are you able to speak in sentences? Do you digress unnecessarily, or forget the point of the question? The time to find out about such problems is before you appear on the lecture platform or TV talk show. It's a lot less embarrassing that way.

Chapter 13

Conclusion

It is interesting that although one of the basic American boasts is "freedom of speech," so few citizens are interested in taking advantage of it. In the large family that is a nation, speech is as important as in our individual families, as a means of communicating and sharing ideas and emotions.

In ancient societies it would never have occurred to the common man—much less the common woman—to make any sort of public address. It was only leaders who were granted such a privilege or who, more properly, took it upon themselves. Mankind may have been on the planet Earth for millions of years, but it was quite recently—only about twenty-five hundred years ago—that Greek communities began to make experiments with democracy. It must then have been taken as self-evident that large numbers of individuals could not rule themselves without developing the art of public speaking.

In the modern age, and in the United States in particular, the ability to address and persuade one's fellow citizens is of special importance. The various components of government—city councils, state legislatures, the House of Representatives, the Senate—are procedural devices set up to accommodate the making of speeches. This is not all they do, but even the creation of legislation could not be accomplished without both public and person-to-person communication. The United Nations itself—though often criticized by conservatives as "nothing more than a debating society"—actually satisfies one of its vitally important functions precisely by being a forum for debate. We do not always get our way in the United Nations, any more than we do in the United States Congress—or, for that matter, within the privacy of our own homes—but the process of communication by speech does help to preserve world peace.

Considering the importance of the speechmaking process, it is interesting that so few are much good at it. John Quick, author of an amusing little book, *I Hate to Make Speeches*, advances an interesting theory as to why most public speakers are inept.

> I think the reason for this is very simple. The majority of people in our society are very boring. They have little to talk about, and almost nothing to think about . . . they are plain vanilla—at home, at work, at cocktail parties—and certainly in front of groups. It is part of the American upbringing to become self-centered, opinionated, and dogmatic, and these aspects do not play well when one speaks to a group of people.

Perhaps Mr. Quick has a point, but then, it never occurs to most of us to make speeches. It would seem reasonable to assume that those who do undertake the task are at least a bit less boring than the rest of us, so I wouldn't worry too much about Mr. Quick's observations.

Don't confuse my suggestions with the Ten Commandments. Every book I've ever read on the art of speechmaking includes a few suggestions that I personally consider ill advised. Art Linkletter, for example, in his enjoyable and instructive *Public Speaking for*

Private People, gives the following rule: Never use notes on TV. "Notes are deadly for a TV appearance," he says, "because the camera sees all."

Art is absolutely right as regards talk-show chatter, but Ronald Reagan has been using notes on television for years and it obviously hasn't done him a great deal of harm. He doesn't use them blatantly, of course, but even in presidential press conferences you often see him slipping the little cards out of his left-hand jacket pocket and placing them on the podium in front of him.

Another way you can use notes on television without being caught at it is simply by asking the producer or director of the program on which you appear to print up your notes on cue cards or a teleprompter device.

Obviously, if you can work without notes on television, so much the better; I simply didn't want you to be put off by the very first word of Art's warning that you should *never* use notes on TV.

Finally, don't expect that reading this book once through will make you an accomplished lecturer. That is no more possible than is becoming a professional pianist by reading a manual on the subject. There's no substitute for experience, in any field of human endeavor. This book of instruction, in any event, should be kept on hand so that it can be referred to as you progress through the various stages of your development. In fact, it might be profitably picked up now and then even after you've achieved your basic ambition and launched either a part- or full-time career as a public speaker.

Index

A

Accent:
  overcoming, 50–51
  regional, 50
Ad-lib speaking:
  avoiding digression in, 95–97
  in daily life, 93–94
  notes as aids in, 94–95
  during question period, 99–101
  sentence structure in, 97–99
  subject familiarity in, 97
  after unexpected introduction, 122–124
Agnew, Spiro, 27
Alcoholic beverages, avoidance of, 60–61
Argument, as form of communication, 18
Attention-getting devices, in speech writing, 19–20
Attire, of speaker, 61

Audience:
  distance from podium, 62–63
  eye contact with, 65
  infant crying in, 120–121
  makeup of, 38–41
  participation, 121–122
  pre-lecture socializing with, 12, 57–61
  response, 87–92
    hostile, 116–119
  small, 114–115
  well-informed, 119–120
Audio tape recorder, as aid to memorization, 52–53
Award, acceptance speech for, 128–137

B

Benefit program, organization of, 161–175

185